This is the Life

This is the Life
Days and Nights in the GAA

CIARÁN MURPHY

SANDYCOVE

an imprint of

PENGUIN BOOKS

SANDYCOVE

UK | USA | Canada | Ireland | Australia
India | New Zealand | South Africa

Sandycove is part of the Penguin Random House group of companies
whose addresses can be found at global.penguinrandomhouse.com.

First published 2023
002

Set in 13.5/16pt Garamond MT Std
Typeset by Jouve (UK), Milton Keynes
Printed and bound in Great Britain by Clays Ltd, Elcograf S.p.A.

The authorized representative in the EEA is Penguin Random House Ireland,
Morrison Chambers, 32 Nassau Street, Dublin D02 YH68

A CIP catalogue record for this book is available from the British Library

ISBN: 978–1–844–88632–6

www.greenpenguin.co.uk

To Tony and Fran.
And to the thousands like them.

Contents

1. The Notebook

For as long as I can remember, the notebook was in the house. Its home was in a drawer beside the telephone, but in reality it was more often than not on our kitchen table, ready to be scooped up at a moment's notice.

A simple, red A6 notebook, just about big enough to fit in the inside pocket of your typical 1980s duffel coat. At the top of every page, my father had written down a year: 1974, 1975, 1976 . . . Then he made a list of boys' names – Adrian Molloy, Ollie Turner, Raymond Walsh – in alphabetical order, in English, and beside that, each boy's date of birth.

My father wasn't a local. He was born and grew up in An Sean Phobal in the Waterford Gaeltacht. By 1979, when he moved to Milltown, a small town in County Galway close to the Mayo border, he had been living for over a decade in Dublin, where he worked for the Corporation. He'd met my mother, who was also working for the Corporation, in the Town and Country Ballroom on Parnell Square. She was from Milltown, and they moved there after her family gave them a site on which to build a house. Their first two children had been born in Dublin, and two more followed after the move. All boys.

What does a thirty-one-year-old man, having just moved west, do to make friends, to integrate into the community? He could go for a few pints with his two brothers-in-law, which he did; and he could join the GAA club. In the early 1980s, those were the two options.

He went to the Milltown GAA AGM at the end of 1980 to see what sort of a club he had married into, got volunteered onto a selection committee for their minor team, and soon was taking teams himself in the younger age-grades. You were, in this scenario, often a one-man band. You took the training sessions, you organized transport to away games, you picked the team . . . and you wrote out the team-sheets.

Every team-sheet required each player's date of birth, and his name in Irish. Because of his Gaeltacht background, Dad knew everyone's name off by heart in Irish, so he didn't have to keep asking lads to spell them out – something a few of the players would have struggled with themselves in any case. For the birthdays, you could either go around and ask every player before every game, or you could keep a record of them yourself and fill it in that way. And that's where the red notebook came in.

So it was that the Milltown under-12 team of 1983 (made up of kids born in 1971 and later) became the first entries into the diary. Three of those under-12s would end up losing an All-Ireland under-21 final to a Peter Canavan-inspired Tyrone in 1992, with Dad as a selector for the Galway team. The project had begun.

My mother's nephew was on that first team, and soon Dad's own sons would start playing under-12 football, but the family connection was almost secondary. The choice was clear: either get involved in the life of the community you've moved to, or remain an outsider. And he was always going to get involved. He was never one to back down from a job. And once you were in the system, in a place like Milltown, it was impossible to check out. Any other sporting interests you may have had did not matter: there was no rugby club, no soccer club, no hurling. It was all Gaelic football, all the time.

Galway is a huge county, but its football heartland is highly concentrated. Everything south of the Dublin–Galway railway line is hurling. There are very few dual clubs in the county. You're either a hurling club or a football club, and that is pretty much decided for you by geography. The area within a fifteen-mile radius of Tuam has powered Galway to nine All-Ireland titles, so it's easy to surmise that that circle takes in more All-Ireland football medals than any other rural area in Ireland outside of County Kerry.

Galway city has provided plenty of footballers to the inter-county team over the years, and Connemara has produced some wonderful players as well, but the mythology of Galway football as languid, elegant, stylish . . . that is provided in the main by the footballers of north-east Galway. From 'The Master', Sean Purcell, to Seamus Leydon of the three-in-a-row team of the 1960s, from two-footed stylists Gay McManus and Shane Walsh to All-Ireland final match-winners Jarlath Fallon and Pádraic Joyce, the area has provided true artists in every decade. This was the hotbed into which my father stepped.

The coaching was a little more haphazard than would be the case today, but the basics were worked on, repeated, perfected. Then, after a few drills, throw the ball in, start the game and let everyone get a touch if they were good enough.

Milltown wasn't, and isn't, a big place. Success would be decided entirely by the vagaries of birth-rates. In 1971 there were fifteen boys born in the village, and it followed that there would be footballers in there. In 1980, there were only six boys born – and therefore not much hope of success for that age group. The notebook didn't tell you much, but it told you that much.

*

Most of the local employment was in farming, and for a time Dad, who had a job in the county council, was one of the very few people going into Galway city every day for work. As Dad settled in the village, word of his daily commute soon got around, and he very quickly became the informal organizer of a village car-pool – though it was not a car-pool in the classic sense, because he did all the driving.

As more and more people inquired about the chance of a lift, he spied an opportunity and traded his Ford Cortina for an orange Volkswagen minibus. The initial contributions towards petrol turned into bus-fare, and it became a little side-hustle of his – and a pretty useful one too for a family running on one local authority official's wage.

The minibus obviously also came in handy for the under-age teams. Every time I meet a player of Dad's from those early years, it never takes long before the minibus gets a mention. It was a reasonably terrifying machine, with seating for twelve (but no seat-belts) and an actual working capacity of many, many more than that. Dad maintains he once headed off to a tournament in south Mayo with thirty-one kids in the back. Some exaggeration seems inevitable in stories of this nature, and yet I have a nagging suspicion this one is true. I have only the vaguest memories of the minibus, but my older brothers must have covered every inch of north Galway in it.

They tell a story of heading off to an under-14 game against Spiddal one evening. The team gathered in the church car park in Milltown, and they only had fourteen players . . . one man short. But Dad had a plan. He landed up to a house on the road into Tuam in which there dwelt a scattering of sons of reliable footballing ability. He hardly needed to consult his red notebook at this stage, but if he did then it would have told him that one of the sons, Gabriel, was thirteen. However, Gabriel was doing the milking that evening, and farming was a serious business in this house.

My brothers remember sitting in the minibus, on the side of the N17, watching the delicate negotiations take place. Tony Murphy wouldn't take no for an answer. After twenty minutes, Gabriel was released from his duties and got into the back of the minibus. Off they went. Marginal gains: they won the game by a point.

My father also used the minibus to drive a crowd from one of the local pubs up to Dublin for big games in Croke Park. He would meet this group outside the Cathedral in Tuam after first mass, and thereafter the schedule ran something like this: five pints in Dublin before the game, five pints after the game, and then five pints on the way home. The bar they frequented, the Red Parrot on Dorset Street, helpfully provided him with a free parking space . . . and why the hell wouldn't they, quite frankly.

Dad would often bring along another non-combatant in the drinking stakes. The two of them would head into Croke Park for the minor game while the rest got lubricated in the pub. That companion was sometimes the Abbey playwright M. J. Molloy, Milltown's most famous cultural export, who presumably had his ears open at all times to the Syngeian bon mots being exchanged between the lads in the back of the minibus.

The whole thing sounds utterly chaotic, but everyone's timekeeping was apparently exemplary. The ringleader was a charismatic figure who ran this boozing band of brothers with an iron fist. Post-match, the arrangement was that they would be out of the pub and in the minibus at 6.30 p.m. sharp . . . and Dad never left Dublin any later than 6.35. Once they were on the road, the plan was to get as close as possible to home before watching *The Sunday Game* at half past nine in a public house somewhere (the village of Mountbellew, about twenty minutes east of Tuam, was often the beneficiary of their largesse).

And notwithstanding the Olympian levels of drinking involved, the only person who ever got sick on these excursions was a seventeen-year-old who joined the crew one year. Rather than having the fifteen pints of porter, he rather unwisely drank fifteen bottles of Lucozade instead . . . which was too much for his teenage constitution. The young man returned the following year and had the fifteen pints of porter without incident.

My father brought me to my first All-Ireland SFC final in 1991, between Down and Meath. We set off early on the Sunday morning, in a car carrying four extremely large fellow club men, and by the time we reached Dublin I was in a state of such high excitement that I could have floated over the turnstiles.

And that was nearly what I ended up having to do, because about fifty yards from the entrance to the Cusack Stand, Dad turned to me and said, 'Now obviously you don't have a ticket of your own [this had been not at all obvious to me], so you'll be sitting on my knee. If the man at the turnstile looks like he's not going to let you in, don't be afraid to turn on the waterworks.' The look I gave him left him in no doubt that this was one job I was more than capable of doing, and with some aplomb.

Being thrown in over the turnstiles sounds like something out of the 1950s, but that's what happened. I wasn't exactly small for my age either, at nine years old, but Dad didn't mind, and I certainly wasn't complaining that I didn't have a seat of my own. I remember snippets of the game – how good Bernard Flynn and James McCartan were, Barry Breen's goal in the second half – but I remember most vividly of all the intense green of the pitch as I caught a glimpse of it for the first time, the blue GAA insignia in the centre and the red-and-black flags of the Down fans on Hill 16, which we were overlooking at that end of the Cusack Stand.

Liam Hayes's brilliant second-half goal happened right in front of us, but I don't really have much of a memory of that. I do remember Colm O'Rourke being brought on with twenty minutes left to try and save the day for Meath.

I also remember my dad's friend Francie Mullarkey hopping out of the car about half an hour after the final whistle, in that warren of streets between the Mater Hospital and Mountjoy Prison, and taking on the role of impromptu traffic cop, directing affairs for ten minutes, expertly breaking the gridlock to allow us to make our escape.

So Dad had four kids under the age of twelve, running around a county the size of Galway attending matches twice a week, taking training sessions all weekend, running a minibus service into Galway every morning, all while progressing up the ranks of the Galway County Council (he would retire having reached the position of County Secretary). It didn't seem daft to me at the time, but it is hard to get your head around now.

When I ask him about it, he obviously acknowledges the implicit role played by my mother. He would work till 5 p.m., drive home, arrive in Milltown at 5.45, wolf down some dinner, and be out the door again to fill the minibus with kids and head off to the next game. That doesn't happen without a spouse ready to do all the heavy lifting, even if there were usually at least two of your own kids piling into the minibus with you.

7

The fact was that Mam was almost as cuckoo about it as he was. She attended almost all the games that were on in Milltown, and she also travelled to plenty of away fixtures, following the minibus with a couple more of us in tow. Having been born in Milltown, she knew every child in the parish almost as a matter of course, and she felt the losses and loved the wins as much as anyone. There were, quite honestly, a pair of them in it.

My eldest brother, Brian, started playing in 1984. I, the youngest son, finished in the minor (under-18) grade in 2000. Over that span of years, my father was in charge of the vast majority of Milltown underage teams. There were certainly more than ten years where he was in charge of all the under-12, under-14 and under-16 teams, regardless of whether there was a Murphy in the squad.

The notebook went on and on. As well as taking over the underage section, Dad became adult club secretary in the mid-1990s, and so he needed more birthdays, going back now to the 1960s, for more team-sheets.

By the late 1990s, when pretty much the entire senior team had grown up playing football under him, the red book existed merely to confirm the exceptional quality of his own memory for figures. Even now when I talk to him about old players, he'll throw in a birthday or two after their names, just to show me he's still got it.

That first under-12 group he took ended up winning three county under-21 'A' titles in a row. After the first of those titles in 1990, Bosco McDermott, hero of the Galway three-in-a-row team of the 1960s, took over as Galway senior and under-21 manager. Milltown were perhaps entitled to expect a selector for the under-21 team. Dad, even though he wasn't involved in the preparation of the under-21 club team, and certainly hadn't asked for it, was chosen by the Galway county board. When I asked him whether he considered saying no to the extra burden the new role would entail, he told me he barely even paused to think about it.

So as well as all the club commitments with Milltown, he ended up spending three wonderful years helping out at inter-county level, watching Brian Forde, a fellow Milltown man, captain Galway to a brilliant Connacht under-21 final win over Mayo in 1992. That was before they lost the All-Ireland final to Tyrone, when an already-balding Peter Canavan inspired his under-21 team to victory.

For me, a football-mad kid, this was the stuff of dreams. Two evenings a week, most weeks, I'd be able to spend time with my hero-father, driving around Galway watching my brothers playing football, earnestly and in painful detail outlining to Dad my thoughts on his team selections. And throughout the summer, Saturday mornings would be spent in St Mary's College in Galway, or in the stadium in Tuam, at Galway under-21 training.

There I was treated like a king. Bosco was a living legend of Galway football, and was a perfect gentleman. The players, young men in college and starting out on their working lives, were unbelievably kind and funny and generous with their time towards a kid who doubtless talked way too much.

After losing the All-Ireland final in 1992, Galway won Connacht again the following year, only to lose an All-Ireland semi-final to a Kerry team managed by Páidí Ó Sé. At this stage my bona fides were well established. Having attended as many training sessions as most of the players, if I kept my head down and my mouth shut I could go pretty much wherever I pleased. And that's how I ended up in the Galway dugout as a ten-year-old, watching Páidí prowl up and down the sideline, utterly terrified by his entire demeanour. He had only retired from senior football five years before, and cut an extraordinarily intimidating physical presence.

There were moments that outlined just how daft and wonderful this life in Galway GAA was. One evening in the mid-1990s, Dad was sitting in traffic trying to get out of Galway city, running late for a game. On the side of the road he saw a fella from Glenamaddy called Terence Morgan, who had played under-21 football with Galway under him, thumbing a lift. For all its fame as a crossroads, Glenamaddy is a pretty tough spot to get to when you're in a hurry.

Now, if Terence was really lucky on the road, he'd get a first lift from Galway city to Tuam; then he'd have to walk about a mile from the Galway road over to the Dunmore road to hopefully get a lift from Tuam to Dunmore; and then when he got to Dunmore, he'd be hoping to spot a neighbour who'd give him a lift from there to Glenamaddy. It was a full evening's work. Certainly when he saw Tony Murphy pull up, he had no reason to hope for anything better than a lift to Tuam.

'Well, Terence, are you heading home to Glen'?'

'I am, Tony.'

'Well that's where I'm going too, I've an under-14 game at seven o'clock.'

I can understand why there's always a big hello whenever Dad runs into him.

Dad left the Galway scene after 1994, when I was starting at under-12 level. (There were twelve boys born in the village in 1982: we had a shot!) He took me all the way through to my last year of minor football with Milltown, when we lost a game against Caherlistrane that we really should have won.

But he had done enough at that stage, and he gradually stepped away once I was done with underage football.

Countless times we walked into our kitchen to hear Dad introduce himself on the phone: 'How's it going, it's Tony Murphy here from Milltown GAA club.' He was always pretty good with names and faces, but I knew he was struggling when he'd greet someone with 'How are they all in Mountbellew?' (or wherever) – this was for when he could remember the fella's club but not his name. Three-quarters of the mail that we received to the house was addressed to *Antoin Ó Murchú Uasal, Runai, Baile An Mhuilinn CLG.*

He was club secretary for years, on top of all the work he did in the juvenile section. He retired from the county council in 2006, and was diagnosed with Parkinson's soon after. He's moving a little slower now than he was, but the GAA is still the centre of his life. He is now his grandsons' and granddaughters' biggest fan. When I go to watch my nephews play for Athenry or Oranmore-Maree and he's not there, people will come over to my brothers and ask where 'the Boss' is.

I think about how much that notebook tells us about life in Milltown in the last fifty years – from 1971 onwards. Emigration has taken a toll, but maybe not to the extent you'd imagine. There are a few names that Dad can't go past without wondering what might have been if they'd stuck around, but the smooth progression of the best underage players onto the club senior team was never really the problem. We just had to produce enough of them.

As the years went on, the notebook also became a repository for the birthdays of characters around the village, to be brought out amidst great ceremony to solve the mystery of how old a person was in the front bar in Mullarkey's pub on some winter's night. GDPR has never been a major concern. The last time I opened the red book, there was a small slip of paper with two birthdays written on it – those of Lionel Messi and Cristiano Ronaldo.

Deaths were marked. Car crashes, heart attacks, suicide and cancer. Young lives taken far too soon, a name beside the names of those peers who were allowed to live on and into soft middle age.

Maybe the most important thing the notebook tells us is that it took until the twenty-first century for the idea of girls playing football to take hold in the village. There are no girls in our family, but I don't think there's any doubt that, if there had been any, they would have trained with the boys every Sunday morning between the ages of eight and twelve. And once Dad had gotten involved at that level, it seems inevitable to me that he would have maintained that connection, even as an overseer.

I know it happened in other villages that girls trained with boys up until the age of twelve or thirteen, but it never happened when I was growing up. No girl expressed an interest, we could say. But the exploding popularity of women's football, the success of All-Ireland winner Aoibheann Daly, the inter-county careers of Máire Ni Bhraonáin and Claire Hehir among many others, suggests that there must have been plenty of latent enthusiasm and ability in the parish just waiting to be discovered and nurtured by a women's football club. A pity it didn't happen sooner.

What was it that fuelled my father's passion? My brothers talk about this a bit. He certainly believed in the GAA as a cultural organization. It wasn't all about football. In the winter months, when the football was finished, he threw himself into Scór and Scór na nÓg, particularly the Tráth na gCeist quiz competitions, tutoring his own sons – and whatever sons and daughters of the neighbours could be strong-armed into competing with us – in Irish history, GAA, and *ceisteanna trí Gaeilge*. My brother John and I have official GAA All-Ireland medals (Celtic crosses and all) as a result.

He admits that there was an element of vanity involved. He was good at it, and he brought success, such as was possible given the size of the parish, to the club. He liked that too – no point in saying otherwise. He would go to the AGM every year and say that he needed help, and others would chip in where they could. My team was lucky enough to have John Concannon, a future Galway coach, helping Dad out when we were at under-16 and minor level. But the wins were often his and his players' alone. Everyone knew that and respected the work that went into it.

In the end it might just have been a belief in young people, a simple joy in seeing them get better at something, and passing them on to the next part of their lives with a skill that had been honed and fine-tuned. He still has an encyclopaedic knowledge of young footballers and hurlers from around the country. Each name is carefully folded away in his brain, ready at a moment's notice to be produced when he sees them on some October afternoon on TG4.

Around four years ago, he was walking around Athenry while staying with my brother Paul for an evening. He stopped to cast an eye at an under-16 team training away in Athenry's second pitch. He came back to Paul's house with a scouting report: 'There's a lad up there, they're calling him Ryan or something – I'd keep an eye on him.' In 2021 that kid made his championship debut for the Athenry seniors, scoring 1-3. And Dad remembers it all.

2. Day Boy

The year was 2003. A Leitrim man of my acquaintance and I were attending a twenty-first birthday party for a girl who was on our course in NUI Galway. If there were fifty people at the party, in her family mansion in Booterstown, in south Dublin, then forty-eight of them were from that subset of society that would have taken a keen interest in Leinster schools rugby. They were all exceedingly polite, but having established our names and connection to our host, their second question to my friend and me was, without fail, 'And what school did you go to?'

I was at least able to report that I went to St Jarlath's College in Tuam, which was a boarding school and so may have existed somewhere on their plane of understanding (even though I was a 'day boy', and so went home on the same bus as every other Milltown kid attending a secondary school in Tuam). My accomplice took great delight in informing our hosts of the grounding in culture and the fine arts he received while matriculating in 'the tech in Drumshanbo'.

This was my first glimpse into a world where the oval-ball activities of two teams of teenagers on a midweek afternoon in Donnybrook was of outsized importance. But I was intimately familiar with the idea of sporting excellence in secondary school.

On that evening in early 2003 in Booterstown, my alma mater still held the Hogan Cup: the trophy given out for the winners of the All-Ireland Post-Primary Schools (or

'Colleges') Senior A Football Championship. Jarlath's in fact had won twelve of the forty-nine Hogan Cup finals played by that time, a scarcely believable win rate for a national competition. But I would have rejected out of hand the idea that my school's footballing prowess, and the whole culture surrounding it, was in any way related to the fevered discussions about the Leinster Senior Cup I heard at my friend's twenty-first.

I moved to Dublin a few months after that soirée, and I started palling around with a few former UCD students who, though big rugby fans, hated the Leinster Senior Cup with a passion. I had never attended a game, but their descriptions – the noise, the colour, the students' ferocious support in the stands – sounded rather uncomfortably familiar to me. Was this not pretty much exactly what went on at Jarlath's games?

Their distaste was about more than just that, of course – it was about the past pupils reliving the good old days on the terraces, the whiff of money and influence and soft power that came off the entire enterprise. And yet . . . it gave me pause. Because the most thrilling GAA memory of my childhood is St Jarlath's run to the Hogan Cup final in 1990.

On that team, along with brilliant players from Sligo, Roscommon and Mayo, were two players from Milltown who my father had managed for the entirety of their young careers: Niall McWalters and Brian Forde. My two older brothers were already students in Jarlath's – Paul in second year and Brian in third – and Paul had even won a Connacht championship medal with the Jarlath's under-15 team in February of that year.

I was seven years old, and I was bowled over by the noise and the colour that the Jarlath's support brought. I'd already gone to plenty of club games in Tuam Stadium, but the colleges games held there felt as though they were being played on a different planet. That support travelled, too. The All-Ireland final that year needed a replay. Both matches were played in Cavan, and even though it all ended in heartbreaking defeat for Jarlath's, the games were extraordinarily entertaining. There were flags everywhere, songs for the entire sixty minutes, and pitch invasions at the end of every game, all co-ordinated by boarders who presumably had little else to be doing in between school and study periods. I remember attending both All-Irelands with Dad, but my brothers travelled on the supporters' buses, which left in a vast convoy from the school gates that Sunday morning. It was a riot of excitement, and I was hopelessly, impossibly hooked by the glamour of it all. It seemed both unbelievable and – with two neighbours on the team, and Paul already playing for Jarlath's – entirely within reach.

All of a sudden, playing for the Jarlath's senior A team became a burning ambition.

When I eventually started at the school, I was named at midfield for the 1st Year team's opening game of the season. But it was all downhill from then on. We lost the 1st Year Connacht final that year to St Mary's of Galway City, by a couple of points . . . and I never did get to play for the senior team. But I was still seen as a footballer in there, still a part of the general gang, which provided a certain amount of leeway.

We would have argued that there was no blatant favouritism at play, but what football gave you was a more informal relationship with a more diverse group of staff members, which inevitably led to a more relaxed approach to discipline than you might perhaps expect. So, yes – blatant favouritism, basically.

I was never very driven academically, and by the time I was

in fourth year I had essentially decided that the most fruitful use of my remaining months in the school would be to attend every Gaelic football match St Jarlath's played, at every level, using my nascent reporting career as cover.

It would usually work like this: I would march up to whatever teacher was in charge of the team in action on that given day, tell them I was covering the game for *Torch*, the school magazine, and more often than not I would be allowed to get on the bus, possibly with a friend or two of mine who would be more than happy to act as umpires. By this time I had already started working weekends as a sports reporter with the *Tuam Herald*, the *Connacht Tribune* and Galway Bay FM, so my bona fides appeared well established, and a well-meaning teacher might even have thought they were helping my future career, instead of just aiding and abetting my escape from double maths on a Wednesday afternoon.

Sometimes these match reports were deemed newsworthy enough to be included in the local papers or broadcast on the local radio, but even if they weren't, the school magazine gave me at least a semi-plausible reason to be missing half-days of school. This sort of thing was indulged far more, quite frankly, than my mother would have liked, but I loved it. And right to the end of my Leaving Cert year, I trained with the senior A team, even though it was clear from early on that I didn't really figure in management's plans.

I was only attempting to follow in the footsteps of so many Milltown lads who had played and won All-Ireland medals with Jarlath's. Nearly every winning team in the school had a smattering of Milltown boys. The village is just fourteen kilometres from the gates of the school, and so when I was there, and for thirty years before then, any Milltown lads going to school in Jarlath's were day pupils – that is, we walked into school in the morning, and walked out at the last bell at 4 p.m., as if it was any other school. In the 1950s and 1960s, however, plenty of Milltown lads would have boarded, cheek-by-jowl with boys from further afield – from Donegal, Sligo, Roscommon, Connemara, and particularly from Mayo.

St Jarlath's was a diocesan school, and much of Mayo fell into the Archdiocese of Tuam, including Westport, Castlebar, and even Achill Island. For the first 150 years or more of its existence, it was seen as a preparatory school for the priesthood, and any young man with a vocation in the diocese gravitated to Jarlath's.

Boarding was an option open to some but not all. Going to boarding school cost money, and not everyone had it. My mother and her older sister boarded in the Mercy Convent in Tuam, but only because they won full scholarships. My grandmother and grandfather decided to send my uncles Jim and Noel to the CBS, because that's where they thought the two sons of a small farmer should go. And day boys were very much in the minority at that time – Jarlath's was seen as a boarding school, and it didn't do a whole lot to attract day pupils, or to change the way it was perceived outside the school walls. It was the one corner of Tuam where even Tuam people might have felt like interlopers.

Talking about this with friends a few years later, I was reminded of an incident I had completely forgotten: an article in the *Tuam Herald* in the aftermath of a Connacht Colleges Senior A final in 1995 between St Jarlath's and their cross-town rival St Patrick's, formerly Tuam CBS. The article was by Ballinrobe man Declan Varley, now group editor of the *Galway Advertiser*. Headlined 'The day the anoraks beat the raincoats', it was written in the aftermath of one of those few rare but exceedingly sweet moments when 'the CBS', as Pat's were still often referred to, were able to get one over on the traditional powerhouse:

> For the neutral observer, this was the dream result; the power of St Jarlath's with their substantial resources on and off the pitch against the down to earth honesty of St Patrick's ... On the terrace last Sunday stood the St Jarlath's past pupils, their expensive raincoats testimony to how life has treated them since they came out of the gates of the College, and year after year they come back to support the team as it traditionally shows the way to the rest of the province. St Patrick's had no such support. Their supporters came in anoraks and hope. The expensive raincoats came in expectation.

It had that priceless, rarely found quality in a local newspaper of managing to annoy every social stratum in the entire town equally. Literally everyone was offended. It was a classic case of an outsider saying an unspoken but universally acknowledged truth, out loud.

Keith Duggan wrote about Jarlath's place in Tuam and in the wider GAA landscape in his first book, *The Lifelong Season*. He quotes the playwright Tom Murphy, a former CBS student:

> They just seemed to have it better. There were strong class distinctions then and the assumption was that anyone who attended St Jarlath's was middle class while the poor went to the CBS. And of course that meant better educational opportunities for them. In my class at the CBS, there were forty-two boys in the class and five of us managed to scrape a pass. We couldn't all have been that stupid.

That was the 1950s. The socio-economic dynamics had evolved by my day, but vestiges of the world Tom Murphy described were still there. Many of my old classmates would get quite a kick out of being described as part of a cosseted elite, but among the boarders of my time would have been the sons of Fianna Fáil councillors and government ministers and captains of industry, along with the sons of big West of Ireland farmers and Garda sergeants – the rural Irish middle classes, in other words.

The language of St Jarlath's could have been lifted directly from *Tom Brown's Schooldays*. There were *monitors* (prefects, basically, but 'monitor' was the word used in the seminary in Maynooth) and *procurators* (a word that was used first to describe an imperial representative of Ancient Rome, but which basically meant 'head boy'); and the boarders ate in the *refectory* (not the canteen). The principal wasn't the principal, he was the *president*. And the school musical was always the *opera*, even when it was *Oliver!* or *Brigadoon*. It felt quaint and even comical, but it was a form of exceptionalism.

It was easier for we day pupils to ignore the issue of class, as Jarlath's was just the local school for us. But there was always a slight residual sense of resentment about Jarlath's in Tuam, something buried in the folklore of the town itself rather than in the hinterlands where I grew up – dating back to the foundation of the school in 1800. NUI Galway history professor and past-pupil John Cunningham wrote a history of the school to mark its bicentenary, and it is clear that from the start the students and teachers of the school were hand-in-glove with the Archbishop's house and the Cathedral, all of which are a stone's throw from each other. The power of the Catholic Church was everywhere to be seen. The sons of rich country farmers walking around a town they didn't grow up in, with an air of authority given to them by virtue of their education and their proximity to ecclesiastical power (for 200 years straight!) were always likely to annoy a few people.

Football absolutely was part of the school's feeling of exceptionalism. The boarders in my year weren't just being sent eighty or a hundred kilometres away to a boarding school, while their friends from national school stayed home and attended the local secondary. On top of this, they were going somewhere that was the best in Ireland at Gaelic football. When I was there, Jarlath's had twice the number of All-Irelands as anywhere else. Your school was literally twice as good at the most popular sport in Ireland as the rest of the country. How could it not feed into how students looked at themselves?

Over the past two decades, all of this has changed. In 2006, Jarlath's ceased to be a boarding school. Student numbers were declining, running costs were rising year-on-year, and with the collapse in priest numbers the school struggled to fill the live-in position of dean.

Three years later, in 2009, Jarlath's amalgamated with St Patrick's, while retaining its name and campus. Pat's was suffering from its own decline in student numbers, and given Tuam had five functioning secondary schools at that time, a little bit of consolidation was probably overdue. For years, some of the best young football talent from up and down the western seaboard had gravitated to Jarlath's. Now, it's a fundamentally different place. As well as the absence of boarders, the towns and villages making up the catchment area for day pupils are dealing with a continuing decline in population.

The new Jarlath's won Connacht schools titles in 2011 and

2012, but the ten years after that, up until February 2022, saw slim pickings indeed. From that scarcely believable average of an All-Ireland title every four years, they went ten years without even winning a Connacht title. The reasons for this go well beyond demographic changes in north Galway. This century has seen an extraordinary democratization in the post-primary competitions.

There wasn't a better story in the GAA in 2022 than St Joseph's of Tulla winning the Dr Harty Cup, the trophy awarded to the best schools hurling team in Munster. A school that had never won a single game in the competition in its history won four ties to lift the famous old trophy, beating recent kingpins Árdscoil Rís of Limerick in the final in a massive upset. It wasn't too long ago that the team from Árdscoil Rís, Paul O'Connell's alma mater, were themselves the upstart story of schools hurling in Munster, winning their first five appearances in the Harty Cup final between 2010 and 2018 before the 2022 loss.

Since the turn of the century there have been nine first-time winners of the Hogan Cup. And there have been five new winners in the last fourteen finals of the Croke Cup (the trophy given to hurling's All-Ireland colleges winners), notwithstanding the continuing excellence of St Kieran's in Kilkenny.

Sending your boy off to go boarding at a single-sex school a hundred kilometres from home at the age of twelve was always a crazy idea, and seems even crazier now. But the residual power of the Jarlath's network in Galway football is still hard to ignore. In Raymond Smith's 1984 book *The Football Immortals*, he describes Tuam as 'a town which throbs with a love of football as Thurles breathes the very spirit of hurling'. This may never have been accurate, but if there was a kernel of truth in it, then it had much to do with Jarlath's. Even when Galway and Connacht football was in the doldrums, Jarlath's continued to fly the flag.

Eight months after Mayo lost the 1993 All-Ireland senior semi-final to Cork by 5-15 to 0-10, and the Galway minors lost to Cork by 4-11 to 0-4 on the same day in the curtain-raiser, Jarlath's were crowned All-Ireland champions. The current Galway manager, Pádraic Joyce, was Jarlath's team captain that day, and two of his teammates, John Divilly and John Concannon, are now selectors with him. And for all that they achieved subsequently, they are still linked by the luminosity with which they played while at Jarlath's, on a team that also included Declan and Tomas Meehan, Tommy Joyce, and Michael Donnellan, who were all on Galway's All-Ireland winning team of 1998.

I gathered with my classmates for our twenty-year reunion in February 2022. On the same day, St Jarlath's played their first All-Ireland Senior A semi-final in a decade. The reunion had been delayed for two years due to Covid, so we were joined by the class of 2001 as well, and I was concerned to see just to what extent the event would be dominated by the football- and football-adjacent crowd in those years. Happily that was not the case at all, and it was gratifying to see with the distance of twenty-two years that it was perfectly possible to have had a good time in Jarlath's without having kicked a ball.

The colleges football match threw in at roughly the same time the reunion was due to start. That could have been a complication. But having stayed to witness Jarlath's fall into a daunting deficit in the early minutes on TV, we wandered off to walk around our old school halls and barely gave the result another thought for the day. Maybe this is where

THIS IS THE LIFE

the GAA schools environment differs from the Leinster Schools Cup. Jarlath's football mattered a great deal to us while we were there, and it matters a bit to us now as past pupils, but far too much football gets played after we leave school for that to ever be the last word for the vast majority of players.

In rugby, by contrast, there just isn't a comparable competitive infrastructure for a huge cohort of players after they leave school. Their Leaving Cert year is, for almost all of them, the most important year of their sporting lives. I was number 30 on our St Jarlath's panel in 2000, and while I might have thought I deserved a slightly lower number than that, that was the reality. I went on to represent my county at under-21 level, and played in a county final with my club. Nicholas Joyce was wearing number 26, and he scored eight points for Galway in a Connacht senior final against Roscommon later in that same decade! Another sub, John Reilly, had coached his club, Kilmeena, to a Junior All-Ireland title in Croke Park a couple of months before we met that day in Tuam in 2022. Other lads on our squad that year would have long and productive careers with their clubs and with their counties too. For us, that year was never going to be the final word.

The emotion and engagement with which we followed our school team while we were pupils got channelled into something else when we left – be that our clubs, our counties, a third-level institution, or a GAA club in a foreign city. There was certainly no question that we would be reliving our sporting lives vicariously through some teenagers, as often seems to be the case in the Leinster Senior Cup. (I keep picking on the Leinster Senior Cup, but I know the Munster Senior Cup has much the same problem.)

I have a friend with rather conflicted feelings on schools rugby: he's basically repulsed by the whole thing, but he also quite likes sporting events in which he has some kind of emotional stake . . . even if the exact nature of that emotional attachment is complex, to say the least. He goes to the odd game to support his old school, which is not one of the major powers, and he meets his old schoolmates, whom he wouldn't ordinarily meet, and he sees how the network helps him and his friends and his family. He sees how his own sister was the beneficiary of free, and extremely useful, advice from a very well-informed school contemporary of his on how to secure investment for her new business, purely because of their school connection. This might not be how we want the country to work, and it's certainly not how he wants the country to work, but there it is.

Any class distinctions at play when I was roaring my support for Jarlath's as a student were certainly more subtle than chants like 'Our dads have more money than yours', or 'We'll beat you in the Leaving Cert' – the sort of thing you hear in Donnybrook every spring. But I can't deny that the distinctions existed, and GAA people can't pretend they have always been the sole preserve of rugby schools.

The academic year 2023/24 has seen girls attend St Jarlath's for the first time. If it feels much like any other school now, then maybe that's no tragedy.

3. Local Hero

I should, of course, have gone to America on a J1 during my time in college. That I didn't owed something to my love of football, something to my cowardice, and something to my attachment to home. In the absence of a J1, I had to get a job. And in 2001, as Galway were slaloming their way through the qualifiers in the first-ever 'back-door' All-Ireland Championship, that job was as a shop assistant in Fallon's Menswear on Shop Street in Tuam.

The shop was run by two brothers, John and Murt Fallon. John had played at right full-back in the 1987 All-Ireland senior semi-final for Galway against Cork, and had scored a point in the dying minutes that nearly got Galway to an All-Ireland final in what would have been a massive shock, only to be denied by a Larry Tompkins free from sixty yards out that earned Cork a replay – a replay Cork then won handsomely. John had also won an All-Ireland colleges title with St Jarlath's, alongside Murt. And having soldiered with Tuam Stars for years, their bona fides as footballers were absolutely assured. But even given their club medals, their colleges medals, and John's senior inter-county career, they were all overshadowed by their younger brother Jarlath, who was the Footballer of the Year in 1998 and – rather uncomfortably for him during the course of my employment in the shop – my all-time sporting hero. But more of that in a moment.

The family were always incredibly well liked and popular, and so the shop was where my dad bought all of his suits . . .

him and, in fact, every adult male within a fifteen-mile radius. My role in the shop was pretty simple. I was encouraged to sell jeans. I could sell casual shirts or sweaters. But no grown man wanted to entrust the buying of a suit, a garment destined for dozens of weddings and hundreds of funerals, to the whims and fancies of a student: only the full-time members of staff handled such weighty consultations.

My cousin Andrew was working in there that summer as well, so we had a good time, and the work was never too strenuous. I was there mostly to sell the odd pair of Wranglers to youngfellas, and to talk football. I was skilled in only one of those tasks, but there was an argument to be made that talking a good football game was the more important skill in any case. The customers were in the shop anyway, and most people appeared to feel that the shop would be in some way insulted if they walked out without buying something: browsing, it appeared, was not something that was done in early 2000s Tuam. All I had to do was point customers in the general direction of what they were looking for, find their size, and keep up a constant stream of chat about the Galway footballers. This was, quite frankly, the role I was born to play.

Throughout that summer and autumn, Galway were embarking on a thrill-a-minute run through the qualifiers, which – this being the first year of the qualifiers – included the almost unbelievable prospect of games being played on Saturday afternoons. I missed the Galway–Armagh game, settled courtesy of a Paul Clancy point in the last minute, because most of the Fallon family had taken the day off for it, and I was stuck listening to it on the radio in an empty shop.

Minding the shop seemed like the least I could do. We all had a part to play in Galway's campaign, and my part was to allow Ja Fallon to feel loved and supported in the warm embrace of his older brothers. For all I knew, the same brothers might well have stayed home and watched the game on TV, but as far as I was concerned I was a key part of the machinery.

Ja regularly dipped his head into the shop, good-naturedly bad-mouthed his brothers to the staff, and headed upstairs for a cup of tea. There are root vegetables less down-to-earth than Ja was, and watching him from my vantage point in the shop was a privilege. As far as Ja was concerned, I was just a young lad from around the place who he'd met dozens of times before, as he had been one of the stars of the Galway under-21 teams my father had been a selector on a decade earlier.

Even before his under-21 heroics, he had been a shining light on the St Jarlath's Hogan Cup team of 1990 I had fallen in love with as a seven-year-old, and there was something utterly compelling about watching him on a football field. Everything about his style of play was spectacular. He was left-footed, a scorer of outrageous long-range points, and already possessed of an almost comically exaggerated jink and dummy solo that was part evasion technique, part epileptic fit.

My clubmate Brian Forde had been captain of the Galway under-21s in 1992 when they beat Mayo in a deluge in Castlebar to win the Connacht title. I was fully invested emotionally in that team, given how much of that year I'd spent at their training sessions, but my abiding memory of that day was not the sight of a Milltown man lifting the trophy. It was of the goal Ja scored to win the game, a bullet of a shot from eighteen yards out.

He had already made his debut for the Galway seniors by

then, and it was absolutely clear that the sky was the limit for him. He was almost obscenely modest, unfailingly polite, and yet universally popular with his teammates.

He was still an under-21 in 1994, but he was unequivocally the inspiration that drove Tuam to the county championship that year. In a family of footballers (there were five Fallons on that Tuam team, including two cousins, Kevin and Seamus), Ja was the jewel in the crown.

As was traditional in many counties at that time, the county champions were allowed to nominate the inter-county captain for the following year, so Ja was made Galway captain for the 1995 season – a role that would have been daunting to many twenty-two-year-olds. Ja ended the season with a Connacht medal, an All-Star award at right-half-forward, and even came within a whisker of an All-Ireland final appearance, only to be denied by Tyrone and Peter Canavan.

Something else happened in 1995, though: the sport of rugby went fully professional. Ja's physicality, drive and imagination could have made him a prototypical number 12 in that code. And he was interested, too. He told me about it during an interview for the *Irish Times* in 2016:

> I probably fell between two stools a little bit, between the amateur and professional eras. Back in 1993 I got a few caps for Connacht, I went to an interpros series in Scotland, which was the beginnings of the idea of a Celtic League I suppose. I was tinkering with it for a couple of years after that, but I gave it one big year in 1997. I was hoping for a full-time contract, but I only got offered a part-time contract by [then Connacht coach Warren] Gatland, so in the end I turned it down. If I'd gotten offered a full-time contract for the year I would definitely have taken it.

As a teenager, I don't remember taking the threat of rugby that seriously when it came to Ja. Maybe the idea that someone born so close to me could become a professional athlete just never really struck me as all that likely. There was also the fact that he hadn't dropped out of the sky – he was from a proud GAA family, and a historic GAA club. He couldn't possibly turn away from all that, could he? That nonchalance was general among the Galway GAA fraternity. Rugby then was not rugby now. The national team was still terrible, and would be terrible for a few more years after that. Numerous club GAA players played rugby in the wintertime with local clubs, just to stay fit, and while Ja was playing at a far superior level to those lads, his career with Galwegians was viewed in the same light. Quite frankly, most Galway GAA people wouldn't have taken rugby seriously as a pastime. But that was how close he came.

That offer of a semi-professional contract came in 1998, and it was only then that Ja decided to return to Gaelic football. It was probably the decisive moment that made Galway the 1998 All-Ireland champions for the first time in thirty-two years. That season was immortalized by the team's substitute keeper, Pat Comer, who followed the team for the year and made the famed inside-the-dressing-room documentary *A Year 'Til Sunday*.

Insofar as that documentary was about football, Ja was the star. The year was broken open by Galway's win over Mayo, who had lost the previous two All-Ireland finals. Ja had been solid and effective on his return to the team after his dalliance with rugby, but he really came into his own in the Connacht final replay against Roscommon. He was so exceptional in that game, and then in the All-Ireland semi-final against Derry, and in the second half of the All-Ireland final, that he was the consensus choice as Footballer of the Year at that year's All-Star banquet.

In the All-Ireland final against Kildare, Galway had started poorly and were three points down at half-time. Ja had been marginally outplayed by Kildare's talismanic centre-back and captain Glenn Ryan in the first half, but the second half was a different story.

Ja kicked the first point after the break, taking on a shot from the left touchline with his left foot that would have looked ridiculous had anyone else attempted it, but which nevertheless dropped with aesthetically pleasing perfection on the roof of the Kildare net. He burned Ryan inside and then out for another magnificent score from play soon after, and then kicked a soaring, majestic point from a sideline ball underneath the Hogan Stand.

His reputation was sealed by those performances. He was a star. But *A Year 'Til Sunday* was about even more than that, and it immortalized him. Inside the first ten minutes of the film, we're in Ja's post van. His route is around his home town of Tuam. He tells us about delivering post every day into Sean Purcell's newsagents on the town square – the same Sean Purcell who had been selected at centre-forward on the GAA's Team of the Century in 1984, and who would be selected in the same position on the GAA's Team of the Millennium in 2000; the same Sean Purcell who was and is regarded as possibly the greatest footballer of the twentieth century.

To hear Ja (the postman) talk about what it would mean to be remembered in his home town in the same breath as a man like Purcell (the newsagent) was to be brought face-to-face with what is for many people the central attraction of the GAA: that ordinary men could do extraordinary things, and that some could experience immortality, all while going about their business among us.

Ja's humility and self-effacement is a recurring thread throughout the film. And in the immediate aftermath of the All-Ireland final, as the players gather in a riot of wild euphoria underneath the Hogan Stand, as it seems the whole county converges on itself in a state of happy ecstasy, Comer's camera picks out Ja, jersey off, completely on his own, his back to the wall. You can imagine the coldness of the wall giving him great satisfaction as – above the fray, in happy isolation – he watches his teammates and his people in the throes of victory.

Later, back in the dressing room, Purcell and Ja embrace. The torch had been passed.

The Fallon brothers lost first their mother and then their father at a young age, and they grew up in the living quarters over the shop, which was run in their father's absence by their uncle Paddy. The shop still bore their father's name for many years after his death, and so the knowledge of their loss remained close to many people's minds.

There was a sense of benevolent ownership then of Ja (and his outrageous talent) by the town, a protectiveness that could have been overbearing. But Ja was well balanced enough to handle it. He was shy, he was humble, and it seemed as if, rather than being bemused by how invested everyone was in his career, he was thankful for the fact that his brilliance as a footballer seemed to be enough of a gift for everyone. If everyone loved Ja, and loved talking about Ja, then it was a relief to him that no one really felt the need to be constantly talking to Ja himself. That was certainly how he preferred it.

As members of a rural club seven miles away, we in Milltown would have had every reason to hate Tuam, the townies. But no one could bring themselves to hate Tuam as long as Ja was playing for them. His aura was all the protection they needed. Having played against him multiple times, on multiple teams that tried by fair means or foul to slow him down or to stop him, I had never seen him provoked into a reaction. He just tried harder, and that was almost invariably enough.

Ja is now as much a part of Tuam's cultural history as Purcell, or Frank Stockwell, Purcell's teammate who scored 2-5 in the 1956 All-Ireland final, a record for a sixty-minute final. Ja belongs to the town in the exact same way that the Saw Doctors do.

When I was nine or ten years old, I decided to write a letter to Sean Purcell. He was a great friend of my uncle Jim Carney, and I knew he had the newsagent's right on the square in Tuam. I wrote the letter, and Sean replied, in beautiful, studied, curiously ornate handwriting. Gerry O'Malley of Roscommon, he said, was his toughest opponent. Winning the All-Ireland final in 1956, he said, was his proudest moment. His advice to me was that I should keep practising kicking with my weaker foot.

And with the letter came a calendar from 1957, featuring a photograph of that All-Ireland winning team of 1956, with each player's autograph printed over their image. It was such a beautiful, thoughtful gift for a ten-year-old, indicative of the nature of the man who gave it. Twenty-five years later, my brother took it from my bedroom in Milltown and framed it, and it hangs in my house in Dublin today.

One of Ireland's greatest jazz musicians, Jim Doherty,

worked in the Bank of Ireland in Tuam in the 1950s, and remembers befriending Stockwell, a quiet, reserved man who nevertheless possessed a capacity for mischief.

One evening the town was awash with speculation over the provenance of a brand-new motorcar that had spent a day parked outside Stockwell's house. He remained tight-lipped on the matter, despite numerous inquiries. Weeks later, over a pint, Doherty asked Stockwell just what the hell the story was with the fancy car. Stockwell told him, in the strictest confidence, that Matt Busby had arrived over from England in search of new players in the aftermath of the Munich air disaster. He felt the only way he could persuade Stockwell to even consider it was to arrive at his door. Having dropped this bombshell, Stockwell swore Doherty to secrecy and returned to his drink. Sixty years later, Doherty told me the same story, and, having been cruelly overserved in the house of Jim's son, the comedian David O'Doherty, I bought it a lot more readily than even Jim did all those years ago.

Ja Fallon managed to be utterly of Tuam, and yet also the property of the entire county.

When we won a league and championship double at under-16 B level in 1998, he came out to present my team-mates and me with our medals. There's still a photo in my parents' house of me posing with Ja. I achieved the rather magical feat of being taller than him while also being absolutely dwarfed by his presence.

Just three years after that medal presentation, I was working on the shop floor below his family home, but the reverence hadn't receded any. In May 2000, Ja had torn his cruciate knee ligament in a club game, and later that summer Galway lost an All-Ireland final replay to Kerry. The lingering regret was that Ja's presence would surely have been enough to have won that final first time round. And so, in that summer of 2001, when I was in the shop, the feeling was that Ja was slowly making his way back to full fitness, and that he would step up when needed.

Customers would come up to me and ask me how Ja's knee was, as if I spent my lunch-break upstairs icing it for him (obviously I would have, if he'd asked). I'd been given a front-row view into the goldfish bowl that he was living in at that time, trying to get back from a horrific injury, trying to regain the intimidatingly high level that he had been at, all while trying to live as normal a life as possible.

There comes a moment before every big game when the final bars of the national anthem are drowned out by the roar of the crowd, and you'll often hear people exhorting their own clubmates in that moment just before the ball is thrown in. I'd like to say that I only started saying 'C'mon, Ja' in the absence of any Milltown man to shout for, in 2001, when I started working in the Fallon family business, but to be honest I had definitely been doing it for a long number of years before then. And while I'm being honest, I might as well say that I do it still, two decades after his retirement.

4. The Sloyan Supremacy

(1)

'The politics of Mayo football would make you sick to your f***in'
stomach. I lived it, that's why I walked away.'

There is a Mayo man of some renown who has allowed himself to be recorded in the midst of various rants against the
ills and evils of Mayo football – its attendant celebrities,
managers, county board officials, and internecine politics.
His name is Jimmy Sloyan. Some of his discourses have been
posted on social media and done decent numbers.

What elevates Jimmy Sloyan above the general run of
agitated supporters is his sporting pedigree: as a young footballer of some repute, he played in Croke Park for the Mayo
minor team. It is not enough simply to have an opinion on
the travails of the Green and Red. It is important for you to
know that you're listening to a man who has walked the
walk, who has done the business . . . at a certain level.

The shadow of this man, and of the vaguely similar characters that probably exist in most towns and villages around
the country, looms large over this chapter – a chapter in
which I, a sportswriter, tell the story of my own playing career. A career in which I might claim to have done certain
kinds of business . . . at a certain level. So with every word
carefully parsed, each syllable checked and double-checked
for hints of vanity, I dip my toe in the water. To abstain from

doing so would mean failing to reflect on the greatest joys and disappointments that the GAA has given me.

I can marvel at the social footprint of the GAA. I can talk to you about how much gratitude I have for the days I spent as a supporter in Croke Park and around the country. But the fact remains that the game is still the thing. I've loved Gaelic football from the moment I started kicking around with my brothers in the back yard. It was the key social outlet of the first sixteen years of my life, and it was the first thing I was good at that wasn't directly related to books or school or other boring, uncool things. It has always been, as John Maughan rather lyrically said of his Offaly footballers in the aftermath of a Tailteann Cup game in 2022, my 'choice of pleasures'.

Our back garden was twenty-five or thirty yards long, and from the age of eight I was capable of kicking a ball the length of it. My father, as I've already related, was coaching the entire village, but he made time for me too. All my friends in national school were as daft about football as I was. It was, I suppose, our chief (not to say our only) mode of expression. I remember a friend and me hitting frees off the ground in the back yard with our bad foot, because it was a skill we didn't have yet, and wanted. We were nine years old.

We won a bit with Milltown teams, and lost plenty more. I played a couple of years ahead, because the years above mine were weak, and I got used to losing. With the kids my own age, we won a Cumann na mBunscol county final, and played in the top divisions whenever possible.

I went into St Jarlath's and made the first-year team at midfield. I scored a goal in Tuam Stadium against St Pat's, our cross-town rivals. (I didn't even see the ball fly into the top corner because my clubmate John Feerick, who was playing at full-back for Pat's, was intent on firing me back up to the square in the town with a shoulder at the exact moment the ball left my foot.)

After that, my career in Jarlath's stalled. I didn't make the under-15 team (the juvenile team, as the grade is known) or the under-16-and-a-half team either (the juniors). And, as I've mentioned, I was nowhere on the senior A panel. But by that stage I had started playing senior for my club, and had done well at early trials with the Galway minors.

(2)

'I was a fine player at the time. A Mayo minor . . . I played in Croke Park, as you know.'

I played a Connacht minor league game for Galway against Roscommon, coming on for the last twenty minutes and doing well . . . and then I tore ligaments in my ankle playing a club challenge game the following morning, and that was that. I would've dearly loved to have played more for my county, or even to have trained as part of an extended panel, but by the time I'd recovered, Mayo had knocked us out of the Connacht tournament.

So I went to NUI Galway, studied Arts (though I did little or no actual studying), and didn't even dream of playing Sigerson Cup, the GAA All-Ireland universities competition. If I'd gone to college as a county minor, or as a starter for the St Jarlath's senior team, then I definitely think I'd have gone out to play for the college. But I had no pedigree beyond the fact that I was a decent club footballer, and I didn't really think I had much business being out there. I had had my chance to show that I belonged on that conveyor belt, and it hadn't worked out.

There was also the fact that there were so many ex-Jarlath's lads, and lads from around north-east Galway, in the college GAA club that it would nearly have been a retrograde step for me to tie my social life in college to football. For many students, playing third-level GAA is a way to meet new people, but for me, the vast majority of my teammates would be all too familiar. It was certainly not anything like a clean slate for me to prove my worth as a footballer – quite the opposite, in fact. That may have been an even more compelling reason for me to avoid football in college than the usual distractions and new-found freedoms of being away from home for the first time.

I had a good season for my club in the 2002 county championship – right up until I had my collarbone broken by the local nightclub bouncer who was playing full-back for Tuam in a league game. I felt I had really started to progress as a footballer, and I got it in my head that maybe I owed it to myself to give the county under-21 team a proper go the following year, my last year in the grade.

That summer of 2003, training and playing with the county under-21s, is the undoubted high point of my football career. Earlier that season, after a couple of training sessions had gone poorly, I wrote down the names of all the forwards in the extended twenty-six- or thirty-man panel that I thought were better than me. I got to eleven. Sometimes I thought about all the schools and colleges games these lads had played in that I had missed. But that was pointless: I was only psyching myself out of contention before I'd given myself a chance.

I remember one evening in Corofin, after a particularly

punishing set of 200-metre runs, lying in a crumpled heap on the ground with the best young footballers in the county, feeling total and utter satisfaction. The sun hung low over the church in the village, the chat among the group was easy and relaxed, and I realized that this was what it was like to be a 'county man'.

I took on more responsibility with Milltown. The high quality of training we were doing with Galway meant I was fitter than I'd ever been, but more than that was the confidence that came with realizing you belonged to a greater or lesser extent with good footballers on a proper county panel. One fed off the other. I played better because I was in with the 21s, and I managed to hang on with the 21s because I was playing better.

John O'Mahony was in charge of both the senior and under-21 squads, and that May, as we prepared for a summer under-21 championship, I trained a few times with the Galway seniors – just making up numbers, of course, but an indication at least that they were satisfied with how I was going.

I remember Michael Donnellan coming over and giving me a big welcome at one of those training sessions, telling me how well deserved my call-up was. I nearly fell over myself telling him I was only there to make up the thirty at training, but he wouldn't have it. I sat in the dressing room afterwards and heard my heroes tear strips off each other. I was in heaven.

As the seniors ramped up their preparation for that summer's championship, they played challenge games on two successive nights, to ensure their entire squad got full matches. Between injuries and absentees, I ended up playing at full-forward against Tipperary on the second night. I was handed the number 14 jersey. Pádraic Joyce's jersey! I scored

1-2, and had a ball until I suffered a minor injury and had to
come off. I ended up getting a lift back into Galway city with
Alan Kerins, and since he was working as a physiotherapist
in the UCHG at the time, he brought me to hospital, and
made sure I was taken straight through to get an X-ray. The
inter-county treatment.

The under-21s went to Sixmilebridge in Clare and played
Kerry in a challenge game, and I scored 2-3. Proper players
score 2-3 in a challenge game and have forgotten about it by
the time they're out of the shower, but it was huge for me. I
remember playing Cork in another challenge game, one where
both counties came with full teams, and I hit the post with a
shot from sixteen yards out that looked destined to nestle in
the bottom corner. Even then I wrestled with 'if onlys'.

I certainly gave the Galway thing everything I had . . . but
I just wasn't quite good enough. There's no under-21 league,
it's just straight knockout, so the year and the Connacht
championship began for us with a semi-final against Roscommon, in Dr Hyde Park. I felt like I was close to being named
in the starting team, and I came on after fifteen minutes or so
for our corner-back, prompting a big reshuffle, which sug-
gested I really was close.

I remember being presented with a goal chance with my
very first touch. I probably should have just fisted it over, but
instead I blazed it into the side-netting. Still, I remember
feeling like I'd done OK. The game was played as a curtain-
raiser to Armagh against Limerick in a Round 4 senior
qualifier, so there was a fairly decent crowd in by the end.
My clubmate Darren Mullahy was exceptional that day, and
so, along with John Devane, Diarmaid Blake and myself,
Milltown had four lads involved in the game-day squad, with
another, Brendan McGrath, on the extended panel. Meeting

my own family and their families in a hotel in the town after the game was a legitimate thrill, but rightly or wrongly I seem to recall taking it all pretty much in my stride.

The Connacht final was going to be against Mayo in Tuam a couple of weeks later, and I remember we played a challenge game against Tipperary without the lads who were also on the Galway senior panel, including Michael Meehan and Nicholas Joyce, two of the county's best inside-forwards of the last twenty years. They were off preparing for an All-Ireland quarter-final against Donegal, and another tilt at Sam Maguire.

The team for that challenge game included a brilliant wing-back named Damien Burke at corner-forward, the idea obviously being that he would come out the field and play as a third midfielder as preparation for the Connacht final, where he would be expected to do the same. The second I saw that, even though I was picked at number 14 for the challenge game that evening, I realized that my goose was cooked. We were going to play just two inside-forwards against Mayo, and I would never in a million years be able to force my way in ahead of Michael or Nicky. I went out and kicked nine points that evening, and I knew it was all for nothing. Maybe I'd have kicked half that if I'd known there was still a realistic chance of me making the team.

I remember the training session two nights before the Connacht final, when the team was going to be named. I was taking frees with Shane Moran from Tuam beforehand, listening to him trying to bet me money that I was going to start, and me telling him I'm 100 per cent not going to get the nod. O'Mahony announced the team, and he felt moved to come over afterwards to explain his decision to me.

I didn't need to have it explained. I'd known Meehan and

Joyce since Jarlath's, and I knew how exceptional they were, but that conversation certainly made me feel better about myself. As it happened, Matthew Clancy, the man who had booked Galway's appearance in the 2001 senior All-Ireland final with a late goal against Derry in the semi-final as a nineteen-year-old, went off injured after fifteen minutes, and I got another forty-five minutes off the bench.

We lost the shagging game by a point. With thirty seconds left I had the ball in my hands on the forty-five-yard line, just to the right of the posts, in an ideal position to swing over the equalizer. I passed the ball to a man in a better position, but he got turned over and that was that. That was the end of my inter-county career.

That moment comes back to me time and time again. Other moments too. There was a ball that came out to me underneath the stand in Tuam Stadium in the final ten minutes, and I will never forget the noise that came up from a crowd of 8,000 people just completely lost in the moment of the tussle. I'd played in Tuam Stadium dozens of times, but I'd never seen it like this – a beautiful summer's evening, another iteration of the Galway–Mayo rivalry in its spiritual home, what seemed to me like a massive crowd, and there I was, stuck in the middle of it. It was an unbelievable experience, and I'd done OK, but that was that.

A kid came up looking for an autograph after the game as I stood around with my family and a few other people from Milltown sympathizing. I was utterly stumped – do I look like an arrogant bastard if I'm standing out here signing autographs after we lost the game, with the number 22 on my back? Instead of just doing it, I refused the kid, and I cringe at that memory even now.

A Mayo player came up and asked me if I wanted to swap

jerseys. I refused that too. If I was only going to get to keep one inter-county jersey for all my efforts that summer, I was going to make damn sure it was a Galway one.

In the showers after the game, Diarmaid Blake said something like, 'It's a fucking sickener, but everyone in this dressing room either has an All-Ireland medal [from the previous year's under-21 championship-winning team] or is young enough next year.' I looked at him as if to say, 'Not me, scan.'

You convince yourself of a million things. If I'd kicked that last ball over, we'd have gone up to Castlebar the following Wednesday, won the replay, and we'd have been able to defend that All-Ireland title. I'd have started the replay maybe, if Matt Clancy hadn't recovered, and between the jigs and the reels I might have somehow held on to my place. I'd have had that chance to join a team photo, to stand shoulder-to-shoulder with my opposite number for the national anthem before a provincial final. Instead, the Galway jersey I refused to swap is a number 22, not a number 13 or 14. Insignificant things like that.

(3)

'I hit him back, with 1-4. One goal . . . and four points.'

A month after that Connacht final, I moved to DCU. Having eschewed the chance to play Sigerson Cup football in Galway, I had the same choice to make in Dublin. It's not like I was on a scholarship or anything – so I had to make the decision to go out and put myself up for selection. But this time, I felt like I had some pedigree. I was a Galway under-21 player. That may not have made any difference to anyone else, but it certainly did matter to me.

I went DCU training a couple of times in October, scored a goal with my first touch in the league, and then injured my knee a couple of minutes after that. By the time my knee had recovered it was Christmas, and I was home in Galway trying to get some money together for the next term. I didn't come back up to Dublin until late January, and when I did, I'd an email waiting for me from the team captain, Bryan Cullen, asking me to come back out training.

I did two weeks of training. They went really well and then, all of a sudden, we were in a Sigerson Cup quarter-final away to Cork IT. I still didn't have any DCU shorts or socks, so I had to pick them up from the sports office the day before the match. As the guy in the office went to look for my gear, I spotted the team-sheet on the photocopier. I was starting at number 13.

I sat in the dressing room the following day listening to Mickey Whelan and Dr Niall Moyna read out the team, and I was desperately trying to remember my teammates' names. I still didn't know them as we ran out onto the field.

We lost that quarter-final to a last-minute point, kicked by the Cork hurler John Gardiner, and it's another major regret. But this time it wasn't just the result that bothered me. So many players talk fondly of their time playing Sigerson Cup. If we'd won that quarter-final, we'd have gotten to play at the Sigerson weekend – the semi-finals and finals were played on consecutive days at a host college. The Sigerson weekend was an experience unto itself, socially as well as competitively, and it would have been cool to be there. I can say that I played Sigerson Cup football, but I can't really say I experienced it in the way that so many others have. Getting to the weekend would have meant another two or three weeks' training, it would have meant actually feeling a part of it, not to mention the fact that it would also have been a massively high level of football to take part in and test yourself against.

For many players, particularly those destined never to reach the highest level, third-level football or hurling is the pinnacle of their careers, a time when they get to play alongside the best of their generation and to make lasting friendships. I didn't have that sense of camaraderie built up among my teammates. I barely even knew their names!

On the back of making that all-too-brief impression with DCU, I was invited for a couple of trials with the Galway senior team, as part of the sort of trawl through the bones of the playing ranks of a county that every manager might do if he didn't like the look of his panel after the first couple of rounds of the league.

I remember taking the call asking me to attend one of those Galway senior training sessions – it was a Wednesday night, and I was in the midst of an hours-long drinking session with my DCU journalism class, having an offensively good time. Galway selector Pete Warren surely realized within moments that he was not on the phone to a young man willing to sacrifice everything for his football dream, but he at least had the good grace not to rescind the invitation on the spot.

That was pretty much as good as it got. Another way of looking at it was that, in a six-month spell between August 2003 and February 2004, I lost a Connacht under-21 final, a county senior quarter-final, a club under-21 quarter-final that might have been the most heart-breaking of the lot, and a Sigerson Cup quarter-final – all by a single point. If I had broken even, if I'd just won two of those, it might have felt like I had something concrete to show for the most high-level period of my football career. But by then I had moved to Dublin, and life, as ever, was starting to get in the way.

(4)

'Know your history.'

I am forty years old as I write these words. I play at inter-mediate level for a club in Dublin, Templeogue Synge Street. A lot of my teammates don't remember Pádraic Joyce as a player, let alone Jarlath Fallon. They couldn't care less about my losing a county final a couple of years after some of them were born. When they ask me what level did I play at, I tell them what I've just told you.

What it adds up to is that I was a solid club player who had some ability but who wasn't a killer. My clubmates who advanced to a higher level were more talented than me, they wanted it more, and they were willing to put everything else to one side to make it.

There's very seldom any mystery about why a player doesn't succeed. John Devane was a year younger than me, but when we were under pressure with Milltown, he was a killer. He scored nine points from midfield in a senior cham-pionship game as an eighteen-year-old in 2002. He won two All-Ireland medals that year, for St Jarlath's and then for the Galway under-21s, before going on to play for the Galway seniors. I didn't have to look too far to find out what the standard was.

But there was one day, in the Galway Senior Football Championship of 2003, when I scored 1-2 or 1-3 in a half of football against St Brendan's in Dunmore. That was a day when I felt like I had the winning of the game in the palm of my hand. I remember I had been picked at right corner-forward, and as I was jogging into my position, I saw a fella my age playing full-back, and I switched with our full-forward because I really fancied it against their number 3. I knew I had a psychological advantage over him, and I asserted it. I was really good that day, there's no point in saying otherwise. And to have had a day like that, even if it was just once, with a big crowd of your own people watching, in a proper championship match – that's a special memory. Inter-county players do it week in, week out, year after year. That's the difference. But it doesn't make the memory of that game any less special for me.

I have regrets about results, of course, but there's not much else I regret – not the effort I put in, and not the effort I didn't put in. When the game asked too much of me, I prioritized relationships, or friendships, or work. If that makes me less of a Fíor-Gael than others, I'm happy to concede that. But in the end I think I played at exactly the level my skills merited. I don't feel I short-changed myself, or anyone else. That in itself is a deeply satisfying thing to be able to say.

5. The Family Business

I was waiting at a hotel in Oranmore to be picked up by the Galway under-21 team bus late one midweek afternoon in 2003. We were travelling south to play a challenge game – I can't recall if the opponent was Cork or Kerry – and, given that this was before the time of smartphones, I'd bought the *Irish Times* to pass the few minutes before the bus arrived.

A couple of other lads were there, north Galway lads, and I had been in school with most of them at Jarlath's. We got to talking about one of our teammates, Éamon Ó Cuív, who'd been playing really well for the last few weeks in training. One of the lads perked up to say that for all his storied background – as a member of the extended de Valera political dynasty – he was a lovely fella, 'even if he does read the *Irish Times*, for fuck's sake'. I started laughing, and he turned to me, saw the newspaper under my arm and said – 'Ah yeah, Murph, but you're different.'

I don't know how different I actually was, but even at that stage I'm sure every player who was waiting for the bus that day had played in a game that I'd reported on for either the *Connacht Tribune* or the *Tuam Herald*. I had been doing two or three games most weekends for the previous six summers, and it put me in a somewhat awkward position, given I was reporting on club championships that I was also playing in.

This is by no means unique, and any young sports journalist who also happens to play a bit will probably find him- or herself in a similar position as they try to build up a portfolio of work in the early days of their career. I wasn't writing opinion pieces, so I didn't have to mind what I was writing too much – they were simply match reports, and anyone who played well got a mention. Also, like every other local journalist, I wasn't really in the business of slating players for individual mistakes.

After that summer with the under-21s I took a Master's in Journalism in DCU, and from there went to Newstalk's *Off the Ball* show on placement, with my best friend Mark Horgan. Six weeks into an eight-week placement, we were both offered jobs there, and off we sailed into a career in journalism.

I was barely in the door when Newstalk won the rights to broadcast the second test of the International Rules series between Ireland and Australia from Croke Park. Newstalk was still only a local radio station for Dublin, so it didn't impinge on RTE's coverage, but it was a big deal for us, and we were eager for it to go well.

My role was as a pitchside roving reporter, and Jim Carney, my uncle, was working the sideline for RTE television, which was a pretty cool moment for us both. I was feeling so relaxed about things that I managed to grab Joe Bergin, a Galway footballer only a year older than me, for a quick interview at half-time, even though I don't recall anything of that nature being decided or signed off on by either Newstalk or the International Rules management. I managed to get a few words out of him as he walked towards the team huddle, where another Galway man, team captain Pádraic Joyce, spotted me and told me to please fuck off at my earliest convenience.

It was typical of Bergin to stop and have a quick chat, equally typical of Joyce not to take any bending of the rules by someone from outside the sanctity of the dressing room, and just extremely funny and surreal to be out in the middle of a packed Croke Park having a chat with a lad from just down the road in Galway for the benefit of a Dublin audience.

I really wanted to play football, but I also really wanted to be a sports journalist. Liam Hayes had managed it, writing for the *Sunday Tribune* while also being one of the best players in Ireland for five or six years with Meath. But if you weren't at that rarefied level, was it possible to do both?

Newstalk robbed me of my evenings, but it did leave the weekends free. Or at least it did until the station won national radio rights for the GAA hurling and football championships in 2011. RTE had first choice of games every weekend, and Newstalk then would get the best of the rest, so while that led to some off-Broadway moments for sure, we also did our fair share of provincial finals – two Ulster finals in Clones, two Munster football finals, a Connacht final, All-Ireland hurling and football quarter-finals . . .

During the 2011 championship I was in Limerick for a hurling qualifier between Wexford and the home team. It was my birthday, and I was waiting at Limerick Junction for the train home after the match, contemplating the universe and my place in it, when I spied Nicky English on the platform. Nicky listened to the show, and had been a guest on a few occasions, but I still would've bet good money against anyone telling me I'd spend my twenty-ninth birthday drinking a few beers on a train with the most iconic Tipperary hurler of the last sixty years.

When Dublin beat Limerick in an All-Ireland hurling quarter-final later that summer, Newstalk had the game live. One of the most challenging parts of my job was to get an interview with a key player or one of the managers after the final whistle. My experience was that it was probably best to attempt this as soon as possible after the end of the game – those interviews were often shorter, often more chaotic, but also more emotional, more truthful, and more exciting for the listener.

These were moments where players and managers had their guard down, when they were in danger of getting swept away in the excitement of it all. Plenty of players and managers were more than happy to tell me to piss off, but I never felt like anyone held it against me, and so I persisted – within reason. The one slight fly in the ointment was that this little to-and-fro I had with managers every Sunday was almost always captured on camera if the game was also being shown live on TV. This inevitably led to my receiving five text messages every weekend confirming that people from all walks of life had seen me getting told to go to hell by various luminaries of the GAA world.

That day in Thurles, I headed straight for the Dublin manager Anthony Daly, who was unfailingly amenable with journalists and who, of course, is box-office whenever he talks hurling, as he's been doing with RTE now for a decade or more. I got to him within about twenty seconds of the final whistle, and I'll never forget him turning to me and saying, 'Jesus, Murph, give me a minute here.' The only slight problem with that was that our commentator Dave McIntyre saw me with my arm around Dalo, and had duly thrown live to me, so I filled the gaps until the Dublin manager had regained his composure and started talking.

The look on his face at that moment was one of confusion, elation, and high emotion. He had spoken to us on the radio show a couple of years before, when he had first taken

the Dublin job, and when Eoin McDevitt asked him about
the 1997 Munster final in Páirc Uí Chaoimh that his Clare
team won, he gave us the most amazing answer, talking about
how it was one of those days that, maybe when you've had a
few pints, you throw your head back, close your eyes and
recall even years later.

I remember thinking in Thurles that afternoon that this
was the kind of moment that I was intruding upon, but it
was such a thrill to be in the midst of all that. Not many
people who fail to fulfil their dreams of playing in these huge
games still get to indulge their fantasies of what it is like to
be caught up in a pitch invasion after a provincial final, as I
was when Donegal won that 2011 Ulster final, or stand at the
foot of the steps in Roscommon behind a steward's cordon
and look out at a sea of humanity celebrating a provincial
final victory.

It was serendipitous that my first experience of working a
GAA sideline – at that International Rules game – was alongside my uncle Jim, because he was the entire reason I became
a sports journalist. Jim Carney was the first presenter of *The
Sunday Game* when it launched in 1978, nearly died in a car
crash, helped manage Milltown to our last ever county title in
1981, returned to *The Sunday Game*, was a selector for a year
with the Galway seniors under Tony O'Regan, and served as
sports editor of the *Tuam Herald* through the 1980s and 90s.
He commentated on TV throughout the summer, with BBC
Northern Ireland as well as with RTE, and as live coverage of
games increased in frequency he was often a sideline reporter
on the big days. There is a ten-minute clip on YouTube of him
in the Cork dressing room after their win over Galway in the
1990 All-Ireland hurling final, interviewing six or seven members of the team and management without a break.

What strikes me watching it now is not just the dressing-room access that was given to RTE at the moment of a team's greatest triumph, but also the vast reservoir of personal knowledge Jim was able to call upon to ensure each chat was tailored specifically to the person he was talking to, not to mention both the respect and the real personal affection the players obviously had for him.

I remember being absolutely devastated by Galway's loss in 1990, but the idea that a member of our family would be intimately involved in the broadcast of the game had already been internalized in some way. And I suppose the idea that I would hopefully one day become a successful sports journalist had also been internalized.

I certainly never remember wanting to be anything else. Jim had and still has a bit of a reputation for being a font of knowledge on the GAA, but what really blew my mind – and the minds of my brothers, who were all very much into movies and music when I was a kid – was that his memory was just as good, and his experience just as varied, when it came to literature, poetry, music or movies. He could talk to us as easily about Tom Waits, Paddy Glackin, Louis MacNeice, or Saul Bellow as he could about Sean Boylan.

I don't really see how a ten-year-old couldn't be swept up by him. He was about as glamorous as the West of Ireland got in the 1980s and 90s. To describe him as a local celebrity wouldn't quite capture it. He was about as well known and constant a presence in the town of Tuam as the Cathedral. And he was famous in that way that Irish television personalities were at a time when most households had only two television channels. He was as familiar to some people as members of their own family – he just happened to *actually* be a member of our family.

If Jim's working career was utterly beguiling to a watching young lad, then his brother Noel, who owned the family farm just a mile from our house, engaged me in a rather more hands-on course in sports journalism. Noel was a precise, clear, fair-minded writer of hurling and Gaelic football match reports for both the *Tuam Herald* and the *Connacht Tribune*. Jim set me dreaming, but Noel gave me the basics.

We had a PC in the house, so on many Sunday evenings I'd be commissioned to type out Noel's handwritten match reports and email them to the *Herald*. When you read report after report, week after week, it very quickly became clear how one could fashion an image of what went on in the game for a reader. What were people interested in? How did the county lads go? If you only had three lines to tell the story of the game, how could you do it? Noel was a master at it.

And so when Jim asked me if I wanted to cover a few games for the *Herald* as a fourteen-year-old kid, I honestly didn't feel overwhelmed by it. Noel had given me a perfect grounding, and whatever ability I had was now Jim's to fine-tune whenever he found the time. It was an extraordinary gift for a young man to have at his disposal.

The first time I saw my work in print was a great thrill. The fact that Jim had barely touched my copy was a far bigger one. And the following week, when he had to almost completely restructure my match report, was an education.

I'd knock on senior club football championship dressing rooms and ask managers for team-sheets. It is a Hollywood cliché to say that it always pays to have an uncle in the business, but in a situation like that, Jim's informal imprimatur was gold dust. And in the years since then, I have met countless people who have told me about Jim's priceless abilities as a mentor, as an encourager of young people, with the uncanny ability to say the right thing to people at exactly the right time in their career.

After I left Newstalk with my *Off the Ball* colleagues Ken Early, Simon Hick, Eoin McDevitt, and Mark Horgan, the five of us set up the *Second Captains* podcast, and did a television show with RTE called *Second Captains Live*: an extremely silly show that nevertheless managed to broadcast some of the best sports interviews seen on RTE television in the last twenty years or more, even if, as they say, it's only myself that's saying it. We even managed to secure an interview with Ciarán McDonald, the Mayo footballer whose theretofore Garbo-like refusal of the limelight made that night a particular thrill.

Things don't always go so smoothly, of course. I wrote a column in the *Irish Times* two days before Galway played Mayo in the 2016 Connacht championship. Galway had been humiliated three years before in Pearse Stadium, and had closed the gap a little in the subsequent years, but there were no reasons to be confident going into that first-round game in Castlebar in 2016. The headline was stark – 'Apathy draining the life from Galway football' – and what followed wasn't much more upbeat. It basically outlined how far behind Galway were, why the county's best players had decided not to play for its team, and the various reasons why manager Kevin Walsh was doomed from the start.

Of course, Galway went on to beat Mayo forty-eight hours later, and while I was celebrating wildly on the terrace across from the main stand in Castlebar, I might also have been mourning the death of my punditry career. Fast forward a month, and Galway were back in Castlebar to beat Roscommon in the Connacht final replay. I was on the pitch at the end of the game with my brother Paul, making my way across the field to where my car was parked.

All of a sudden, in the midst of the celebrations, I found myself face-to-face with Kevin Walsh, who looked at me, walked away ... then turned around, looked at me again, shook his head and walked on. If my brother hadn't been there to witness it I'd have doubted my own eyes, but really there was no doubt about it. If he hadn't read my column, he'd certainly heard about it, and he really, *really* hadn't liked it. And if he had properly wanted to lord it over me at that moment, he'd have been well within his rights.

That's the risk you take when you enter GAA journalism. There's no point in trying to stay popular with your own crowd if you're going to be covering them, because in the end no matter how much you equivocate, it'll never be enough. Better to acknowledge your biases, be as honest as you can be, and let the cards fall where they may.

For all that one's attachments make themselves apparent in conscious and unconscious ways, I still feel more qualified to talk about Galway than any other county. And this feeds into a wider argument that rears its head every summer, about RTE having people from the counties involved in their live games acting as pundits.

Some argue that only 'neutral' pundits should be chosen, but I disagree fundamentally. For one thing, the very nature of the GAA basically ensures that no one from outside any county will know half as much about a player's prior history as even an averagely tuned-in supporter of that county. (It's important to say here that many pundits do try to bridge that gap by talking to local journalists and local radio analysts. The best ones put in that hard work, but it's still no substitute for first-hand knowledge.)

The summer of 2021 was a particularly fraught one for analysts trying to balance a serene life at home among their own with their work at a national level as RTE pundits. Sean Cavanagh and Pat Spillane had an almost entirely nuance-free slanging match before Kerry and Tyrone's All-Ireland semi-final, over the Covid outbreak in the Tyrone camp that necessitated a week's delay in playing the game, while Kevin McStay was hauled over the coals by his own people for not sufficiently denouncing on co-commentary the tackle by Dublin player John Small on Mayo's Eoghan McLaughlin, which left McLaughlin with a broken jaw.

Cavanagh and Spillane's set-to happened a week after McStay had tried to clarify his position on the tackle on *The Sunday Game* highlights show (and again in print in the *Irish Times* the following Tuesday), to no avail. So maybe they had been warned. Some of the abuse McStay took from Mayo people was laughably over the top. The message appeared to be that everyone should call it as they see it . . . unless they're talking about one of their own, in which case, they should get that jersey on and play their part. The lesson learned by Spillane and Cavanagh might have been that, while thirty-one other counties might blanch at one's biases being so clearly laid out, the county you actually live in is the only one where that reaction really matters.

In any case, there's been a definite shift in sports broadcasting generally towards pundits-as-fans, not away from it. On Sky Sports' Premier League coverage, there is the Man City one, the Man United one (or two), the Liverpool one (or two), and they're expected to act as a conduit for the emotion of the audience. They're selling the spectacle of sport back to us in the way most of us live through it – as an emotional rather than an analytical experience.

So the people who say that TV punditry has moved on, and RTE needs to move with it, have it slightly wrong too, I think. Gary Neville and Jamie Carragher are very good at analysing games, but that's not the only reason I find them compulsive viewing. They like correcting each other, they enjoy taking each other down a peg or two – and they respect each other's opinions enough to laugh at each other and genuinely challenge each other.

They absolutely do not hide the fact they played for Manchester United and Liverpool for a combined total of well over thirty years. It appears to me as if they're encouraged to ramp it up. They've made missteps as they try to tread that line, but bias isn't the problem. We're all biased. We all have attachments. If you're entertaining and educating us as you go, we won't even care.

I'm sixteen years old, and I'm gazing anxiously out of our front window on a beautiful sunny summer Sunday morning, waiting for Jim to drive through our gate.

'He told me last night that his throat is sore, so be prepared for him to say nothing to you on the way down,' my mother is telling me. I'm heading to Thurles to watch him commentate on Cork against Waterford in the Munster Senior Hurling Championship.

I have a job too, on this occasion. I'll be marking out the wides and the point-scorers on Jim's programme as he's commentating. Two hours of complete silence as we make our way through the back roads of south Galway is a price I am more than willing to pay to experience what it's like to make *The Sunday Game*. Jim arrives, I sit in the front seat and he reiterates the parlous state of his vocal cords . . . before talking to me non-stop for the next two hours.

We arrive in Thurles in plenty of time and Jim slowly manoeuvres his way through the game-day throngs and past the Garda barricades to a parking space behind the stand. The fans walking in to see the start of the minor game are a little bemused by the idea of a car following them on the road this close to the back of the stand and turn in slight annoyance to see who is crawling up behind them. That annoyance turns to recognition and then paroxysms of joy when they see that it's RTE's Jim Carney. As he tries to parallel park his car beside the TV trucks, there's a group of auld fellas gathered around advising, cajoling, directing, and silently judging Jim's parking technique.

As Jim gets out of the car he's beset by these men and the questions start coming. Are Waterford going to do it? How are Cork shaping up? There can be little doubt but that these headbangers know more about it than even Jim does, but Jim's word is gospel. 'I met Jim Carney outside and he says Cork have a right chance' are words I have no doubt will be repeated, and more than once, over the course of the next three hours.

We make our way to the open concourse of the Old Stand in Thurles, and then out to where the big field reveals itself. Up to the back row of the stand then, and a rusty nondescript old iron door is opened and we walk up to the gantry.

The gantry leads up and out until it seems like you're almost suspended in mid-air above the pitch – it's the most wonderful place to watch a game from. Jim outlines my particular role, introduces me to the cameramen, and then he gets to work, nervously checking and double-checking his notes. There's obviously no laptop, no real connection with head office, and since the game is not being shown live, no co-commentator. It's just a man, his notes, his rather-too-tall-for-his-age nephew, and a microphone.

I wonder if Jim will watch back the highlights package they end up broadcasting tonight, or if he's happy to just get the job done and then let the editors do their work. I try to imagine myself doing this job, and I can't. I wonder if Jim will look at me as he's talking, just so he feels like he has an audience and isn't just speaking to the ether. But his focus is completely on the field of play. If I have something to point out to him – the number of wides, or the amount of scores a certain player has racked up – I point to the programme in front of him where I'm tallying such things. The focus required by Jim is stunning to me.

The game itself is typical blood-and-thunder Munster championship fare. Cork's Mickey O'Connell scores eight points from play in a 0-24 to 1-15 win. I'm pretty sure Jim makes some reference to 'a magnificent seventh' after his second-to-last point, as I hold up seven fingers, but everything else from the broadcast is lost to my memory, and certainly I'm sure from Jim's, given this was just another summer Sunday on the road for him.

Somewhere around Gort, engaged in some argument with his own memory, Jim overtakes a very slow-moving car about 300 yards from a right turn. Taking his time swinging back onto his side of the road, he runs over the first twenty yards of the rumble strips that signified the right turn was coming up, and that you should vacate the middle of the road to allow a car room to stop completely and wait to turn off.

Out of nowhere a Garda car appears in our mirrors. Jim pulls in and the Garda approaches the window. 'Well now, did you know you just drove over the hatched lines there?'

Jim's immediate response is, 'The hatched lines? Well I've never heard that phrase before in my life! The hatched lines . . . well that beats it all now.' The Garda, who had been maintaining an officious aloofness, notices something in the voice, looks a little harder at the road-user in the dock in front of him . . . and realizes who he's looking at. 'Ahhh, Jaysis, Jim, it's yourself. Are you on the road home from Thurles? Are Cork the real deal this year?'

For the *Tuam Herald*'s 150th anniversary in 1987, Jim wrote a startlingly good piece about how he started in journalism: how he was an extra in *Alfred the Great*, the Anglo-Saxon epic shot in north Galway in 1967; how he grew the best beard in the 'junior peasant extra' section; how he slept in a barn after spending the winnings of said competition in Canavan's of Belclare; and how a couple of weeks later, as he pondered what he wanted to do with his life, he was approached by the editor of the *Tuam Herald* at the time, J. P. Burke, and was offered a job.

He described his career since that moment thus: 'It was the start of something good, which has lasted.'

And in ways too innumerable to mention, that was the start of my journey to sportswriting too.

6. The Year of Living Conveniently

In the year 2005, for the first time since my very early childhood, I didn't kick a single ball in anger in an organized Gaelic football game. I was twenty-three, I was living in Drumcondra in Dublin, I had my first full-time job, I was supposed to be rehabilitating a cartilage injury to my left knee that had necessitated an operation the previous year . . . and I was having the time of my life.

That knee injury – sustained during a humdrum challenge game in Tuam – gave me all the cover I needed to step away from football at the exact moment that the possibilities of Dublin were revealing themselves to me. On top of that, the injury came along at a time when I was feeling a certain level of disaffection with the game – of which more anon – and after a summer of not thinking about football much at all I was unwilling to do the hard work required to make sure the knee healed quickly. And by the time it did eventually heal, I had filled my life with other interests.

I had a job I was enjoying immensely on *Off the Ball*. I also had a second job, as a fact-checker and breakfast-roll collector on an RTE TV show called *Park Live* that was broadcast live from Croke Park on Sunday mornings before that year's big games. There was no way to do that job *and* get to Milltown for games. The *Park Live* job gave me a unique insight into how to make live television. But my sphere of responsibility was laughably small, and if the desire to play football at home had really been there, I could have passed up the job without a second thought. The reality was that I just wasn't ready to give up every weekend of my life to go home to Galway and play club football.

So what was my relationship with the GAA at this time? I lived literally around the corner from Quinn's Pub, and so just a couple of well-hit forty-fives from Croke Park itself. Like my father before me, who had lived on Clonliffe Road with fifteen other men in a lodging house when he first came to the city in the mid-1960s, I took full advantage of my proximity to the Big House.

My first game of the year was Dublin against Longford on the Hill in Round 1 of the Leinster Senior Football Championship: still the only time I have ever been on the Hill for a Dublin game. It was fairly sparsely populated that day, and I was only up there because my colleague Eoin McDevitt was making a radio documentary about the last Dublin team to win the All-Ireland, ten years before, in 1995.

I went to see both Leinster finals that year, as well as the Ulster football final, and every hurling and football quarter-final in Croke Park that summer (including replays). I had a GAA press pass that wasn't *technically* a guarantee of entry for games of this magnitude, but there was something about being able to land up to the press entrance – safe in the knowledge that if I was refused entry I'd be back on my couch four minutes later watching the game on television – that made me hard to turn away.

The press pass took care of most of the quarter-finals. I needed tickets for the semi-finals and finals – the power of the press pass did not extend that far – but that was OK: for the first time in my life I had some money and was not excessively burdened with overheads. I didn't start out on a mission, but certainly by the time the All-Ireland football final came around I felt I couldn't miss out on completing the set.

Long before that, on a Wednesday in early July, I received a rather strange request from a friend of my brother who worked for the Galway Film Fleadh: 'Would you be able to get two tickets to the Leinster hurling final?'

Given this would be a game attended by no more than 45,000 people in a stadium with a capacity of 83,000, I felt this was a task well within the compass of the Galway Film Fleadh, but they were obviously looking for a couple of free ones. So I said yes, that's probably something I could do, before being told that the tickets were for Paul Schrader, the man who wrote the screenplay for *Taxi Driver* (and lived most of it, too).

This was a bit out of the ordinary. Schrader was generally regarded as one of the crazier individuals working in American cinema in the 1970s and 80s, and having seen *Taxi Driver*, *Raging Bull* and *The Last Temptation of Christ*, as well as some of his own directorial efforts, I was excited to meet him. But the Film Fleadh people told me that I was not to sit beside Mr Schrader, and not to talk to Mr Schrader either. It was a surprise that I wasn't forbidden from looking Mr Schrader in the eye as well.

The Film Fleadh apparatchiks were given the unenviable task of picking up the tickets, which I had successfully winkled free of charge from one of the GAA's main sponsors at the time, at around 10.30 p.m. on the Friday night before the Leinster final. At that moment in time, I had been once again cruelly overserved in Sin é, a pub on the northside quays, and when the festival people rang me to say they were outside I promptly gave them a piece of my mind – informing them that I would be there in the Lower Cusack in my *professional* capacity as a journalist, that I would, contrary to instruction, sit beside one of American cinema's great iconoclasts, and that I'd be reddening the ear of the Wexford right-half-back too if I felt he wasn't pulling his weight, as is the God-given right of the free-thinking Gael. I told them where they could stick their free tickets if they didn't like it. They took the tickets, possibly wondering if they might just have overplayed their hand.

I showed up on the Sunday feeling rather less strident, took my seat, and had a few moments of quiet conversation with Mr Schrader and his young teenage son, who looked epically, comically, galactically bored by the entire affair. Did the man from whose imagination sprang Travis Bickle and I gasp in simultaneous wonder at Eoin Quigley's first-time pull from the halfway line that went over the bar that day for one of the great scores in modern hurling history? I'd like to think that here was a moment of such transcendent beauty that Schrader and I reached across the invisible barrier erected between our cultures and shared a moment of tortured human connection . . . like that last scene of *American Gigolo* he stole lock, stock and barrel from Robert Bresson (not that I mentioned that on the day). However, my precise memory of that shared experience is cruelly lost to the sands of time.

Other days in Croker that summer were a little less dramatic. I watched Galway beat Tipperary in the All-Ireland hurling quarter-final with a group of friends from college. These included an old flame of mine who had once dated a Tipperary hurler, and whose time with me may indeed have overlapped ever so slightly with her time with the Tipperary hurler, leading to an extremely comical evening in the GPO nightclub in Galway city as he searched in vain for his love rival.

I went to the drawn game between Dublin and Tyrone in the football quarter-finals by myself, and was rewarded for this with a ticket in the front row of the upper deck of the Davin Stand, which gave me an unrivalled view of Owen Mulligan's wonder-goal that day. I brought a Tyrone girl of my acquaintance, from the Unionist tradition, to the replay. She was a little late getting there, and I may not have noticed her reticence as we rushed to our seats in the Upper Hogan. After ten minutes I realized Gillian hadn't said a word. I tentatively inquired as to her general well-being.

'I'm just . . . this is a little overwhelming,' she said as she looked down at the vast heaving mass of humanity on Hill 16. 'I'm used to going to games in Windsor Park.'

I remember my first look at Croke Park, before the All-Ireland final of 1991, and I'm certainly glad my father gave me all the time I needed to drink it in. I wish I could've done likewise for the woman who'd become my wife nine years later.

Gill was there for the final too, and as we walked across the pitch from the Cusack to the Hogan Stand, so we could get out onto Jones Road and home, she spotted a few other people from her side of Cookstown who, shall we say, were banking on not running into anyone else from her side of Cookstown, having a whale of a time for themselves listening to Brian Dooher's captain's speech.

Galway had lost the All-Ireland football quarter-final to Cork, a game that marked the coming-out party for Michael Meehan and Sean Armstrong, who had already won an under-21 All-Ireland earlier that summer and were scoring for fun at all levels. Hopes weren't high for our hurlers in the All-Ireland semi-final against Kilkenny, indicated most decisively by the fact that no member of my family came up for it. I ended up watching the match with my aunt Mary, who lives in Glasnevin and who's been to more Galway All-Ireland finals in hurling and football than anyone else I know. Up until 2022, she hadn't missed one since she moved to Dublin in the mid-1960s. That's quite a few when you consider all the football finals we lost in the 1970s, all the hurling finals we reached in the 1980s, and the various successes of the last twenty-five years.

Aunt Mary's apartment is where most of our big days out as Galway fans begin. It's where my brother brought his future wife to meet his family, before the 2001 All-Ireland football final. Given there were probably nine or ten of us in a small apartment sitting room at the time, it might have been quite a stressful afternoon, but we were all too busy getting insanely nervous before the game to pay attention to the newest member of the family silently judging us all.

I recall gathering in that sitting room for another big game, possibly the 2015 All-Ireland hurling final, and starting the holy sacrament of divvying out the tickets to ensure everyone got put in their designated spot. Mary started speculating as to where exactly in the pantheon of great All-Ireland final tickets the one she had just been given lay. (None of us have to wait until we get to the ground to see how good the ticket is – Croke Park's exact seating plan has been seared onto our brains for at least the last fifteen years.)

She was able to recite, almost unbroken, the exact location from where she watched every All-Ireland final that she'd attended in the half century she'd been going to them supporting Galway – the ticket for the 1981 All-Ireland hurling final ('and that fecker Johnny O'Flaherty') was a particular stand-out, apparently.

It would, of course, be hilarious if I could just write this off as the crazed rantings of a deluded family member . . . but then my father and my mother and all three of my brothers were also capable of pretty much nailing to within ten yards where we'd sat for every All-Ireland final we'd attended as well. 'Well, I watched the 2001 hurling final from the front row of the Lower Cusack, section 307, and I actually enjoyed it – I got a great view of Fergal Healy's goal from down there,' were some words that came out of my mouth that day, fourteen years after the event in question. There are people who arrive late and leave games early, and then there are people like us. We don't feel superior, nor should we. It's just the way we are.

In any case, in 2005, given it was just Mary and me in a rather thinly populated Croke Park, we had plenty of room to throw ourselves about. And that's exactly what my aunt did, elbowing me with greater and greater ferocity in the ribs as first Galway and then Kilkenny went goal-crazy. The game finished 5-18 to 4-18, and I was able to inhale and exhale without wincing in pain just in time for the All-Ireland final three weeks later – a game that Galway never really looked like winning against Cork, and didn't.

That summer contained multitudes: the Ulster football final held in Croke Park; a shift in the balance of power towards Tyrone; Sean Óg Ó hAilpín's victory speech *as Gaeilge* as Cork went back-to-back. But it was also a perfectly average GAA summer, and that was fine with me, living, as I was, a few minutes' walk from the best GAA in the country.

I had two more summers in Drumcondra before I upped sticks for Stoneybatter, and then the Liberties, but they weren't quite like 2005. Maybe it was because I had a girl-friend, and then a wife, from that summer onwards. Also, I was back playing competitive football the following year. Maybe it was just an itch that I had comprehensively scratched. Or maybe watching Kilkenny narrowly defeat Wexford in a run-of-the-mill Leinster hurling final with an almost completely mute Hollywood firebrand was a spectating highlight I could never hope to top. Either way, it was the high life.

7. The Rocky Road

In late 2005 I met my old DCU Sigerson coach, the redoubt-able Mickey Whelan, at a press conference I was covering. Mickey asked me was I playing any football. I told him no. He said, 'That's really not good enough,' and he asked me to come training with St Vincent's, where he was in charge at the time.

I hadn't played for Milltown in either of the previous two years. I loved life in Dublin maybe more than I'd ever expected. Now I had a choice to make: either to play with Vincent's or not to play at all. After a fair degree of soul searching, I joined them for the 2006 season.

In theory, this should have been much more manageable than trying to play for Milltown, but in reality it was still far from ideal. *Off the Ball* was on from 7 to 10 every weeknight. My working day ordinarily began at 2 p.m., and I was usually on-air live every night from 7 until 7.25 with an extended sports bulletin. Between then and 10 p.m. I'd often be researching and booking guests for the following day's show. But when I could get out early to make training on Tuesday or Thursday nights, I'd hop in a taxi at 7.30 and hope to be in Marino for the start of the session at 7.45. Realistically, given it was putting my co-workers in a bit of a spot, I could only ever attempt to make one midweek session, and I was still frequently late and stressed before I'd even made it onto the field.

Of course, we trained every weekend as well, and I enjoyed

that, and everyone at Vincent's was really welcoming and supportive. But when the only person who knows you in a club is the manager, and you're missing at least one session every week, it's pretty difficult to argue your case for a starting position.

I played a few league games, and I remember kicking a point as a sub in an early championship game, but it couldn't last. Having joined in February 2006, I had stepped away again by September of that year. St Vincent's were operating at a really high level, and I felt like I was taking the piss – and that's not really the sort of fella you want to have around. It certainly wasn't the sort of fella I wanted to be. All it had really told me was that playing the sport was still something I loved, but this wasn't the answer.

I went home to Milltown for Christmas 2006. In a nightclub in Tuam, I was drinking with some friends from home when a few of them – not all of them by any means, but a couple – registered their utter disgust at my decision to 'walk out' on my club and its up-and-coming group of players. I had played county under-21 for Galway. I was supposed to be a significant part of the team for the next few years. And I was nowhere to be seen.

My colleague Ken Early said to me once that the GAA runs on emotional blackmail, and it's hard to argue with that characterization. I could have written off the Tuam nightclub intervention, but it was definitely a little uncomfortable. A few days later, a member of Milltown's senior management, a man I really respected, called to the house. There's no doubt the two episodes were entirely unconnected, but I'd been stung by the criticism from my peers, and had thus effectively been softened up for the visit of this emissary. He spoke of the confidence the coming year's management had in what we could achieve, and my potential part in it, but that was really beside the point. Feeling like a heel, or even being made to feel like a heel, was not a position I enjoyed. So I rejoined Milltown. And from the moment I made that decision, I knew I'd made the right choice.

There was a bit of backstory I haven't mentioned. In the months before I moved to Dublin, there had been some wrangling about the Milltown senior team management and the executive of the club. I found myself on the opposite side to most of my teammates, and I was a naive twenty-one-year-old who didn't handle himself very adroitly. I think I carried my discomfort about this around for a lot longer than the players on the opposite side, and I allowed the situation to drift while I was out injured and making my way in Dublin in 2004 and 2005. There was never any outright unpleasantness, but a general silence fell upon proceedings as I spent those two summers away from the club.

Perhaps then I believed that I could join Vincent's without a second thought, and that my absence would barely be noticed. That wasn't the case, and in the final analysis I'm thankful for that. At the same time, I think that there was a very good chance I'd never have played again if I *hadn't* played that year in Vins. The experience, unsatisfactory though it was, had maybe focused my mind on the fact that the game itself was something I loved.

For some people in Milltown, my absence in 2005 had been a case of indolence – frowned upon, but certainly acceptable. The decision not to play for a summer (or two) was one that could be reversed simply by showing up at the pitch in Milltown, togging out and rejoining the group. Joining another club was seen as another, far more definitive statement of an intention to leave Milltown in the past – a clean break, rather than a hiatus that could be quickly ended.

This is not an uncommon mode of thinking. There are plenty of absolutists out there who believe that you play with the club you were born into – end of story. That's still the experience of the vast majority, and it is one of the central tenets of the entire association. If I find myself ever explaining the GAA to someone from outside the country, it'll be the first thing I'll say: 'It's amateur, and you play with the lads you grew up with. And if you're good enough, you play with the county you were born in.'

This is everyone's dream scenario . . . until the dream ends and life gets in the way. The harsh reality for many people, particularly on the western seaboard, is that the job they want – or the job they can get – is nowhere near where they live. If football is the only thing tying you to home, is that alone worth sacrificing your employment prospects? Is it worth spending all your free time on the road, travelling to training and matches? The answer, in any logical world, is that this isn't a question even worth asking. It can't be. But in the real world it has been something plenty of people have done.

I realized that if I was going to work in sports journalism and commit myself entirely to it, I would have to live in Dublin. I knew, too, that the GAA has been at least partly to blame for plenty of Dublin life stories never getting off the ground. I've seen them, and worked with them – lads who come up to Dublin, live in a house-share with people they barely know, get the earliest train back every Friday, get the latest possible train back on Sunday, barely go out during the week and do all their socializing, as well as all their GAA playing, at home at the weekend. They never give Dublin a chance. Then they move home after college, after a place-ment, or after two unhappy years in Dublin, and they say 'never again'.

There are obviously others who adapt better, who throw themselves more willingly into making a life in the capital (or Cork, or Limerick, or Galway). They are also the ones more likely to call a halt to the constant up-and-down of playing with their home club and transfer to a club where they now live.

But this is rarely a choice that anyone is happy to face. It is, in fact, often the trickiest decision that many of these young people will have to make before they turn thirty. There are times when it's driven by bitterness, or by a row that erupted in their home club, and those decisions certainly aren't easy. But far harder are the decisions you make because it just . . . suits you better.

I tried to avoid the emotional blackmail. I recently asked some of my peers in Milltown if I'd given them any heads-up that I was about to join Vincent's. They told me that, to the best of their recollection, I hadn't breathed a word to them until my mind had been made up.

I barely even consulted my father. As is sometimes the way when you're twenty-three, you think that you can shed your past lives like a skin. And sometimes you can. But I still regret moving to Vincent's, for the simple reason that I was just running away from a thing that was a couple of conver-sations away from being definitively buried between my clubmates in Milltown and me. And that was how it turned out. Christmas 2006, and that combination of the carrot and stick, was all that needed to happen.

I realize that 'regret' seems a big word, given that I'll defend to the death a player's right to move to a club in whichever city or county he or she happens to be living in.

But the logic of that position doesn't make the actual deed any easier. 'You play with the club you were born into' is a uniquely powerful formula in the GAA. A step across that Rubicon is never one that a player takes lightly. I tried to take that step and not look back, but the ties that bind were much deeper and more meaningful to me than I'd thought.

Rejoining Milltown involved an implicit commitment to throw myself into the team's preparations for the coming year. My brother Brian got married in April 2007. After that, I was where Milltown GAA club wanted me to be every weekend.

I was twenty-five years old, I didn't have a car and couldn't have driven it anyway, I was in a relationship, and I spent every single weekend that summer getting the morning train west to Athenry or Claremorris. If it was to Athenry, I'd walk to my brother Paul's house and he'd drive me to Milltown after feeding me or otherwise amusing me for a couple of hours. If my train was to Claremorris, Mam or Dad would pick me up and bring me back to Milltown. Oftentimes, we wouldn't train until Sunday morning, which meant Saturday nights at home with my parents, or a couple of sneaky pints in Tuam. If we'd a game on Saturday evening, then I could have my few pints in Tuam guilt-free and head back to Dublin next morning.

But every weekend started the same – pack up the boots, walk to Heuston, buy the *Guardian* and the *Irish Times*, get on the train, and then do the same thing in the opposite direction thirty-six or forty-eight hours later.

To friends of mine with no interest in the GAA, that level of commitment seemed deranged. To my teammates and coaches, it was the bare minimum. They would not have been out of step even with serious club teams at that time if they had asked me to return to Milltown for one of their two midweek sessions on Tuesday and Thursday nights. Plenty of club players were doing it then, and are doing it now.

That was something I could easily say my job precluded me from doing, as we were a night-time radio show after all. Any time the lads in Milltown asked me about what I was doing to make up the deficit in training, I'd say, 'I'm doing a bit up in Dublin,' which would seem to suggest solo fitness work every morning before work, but which very quickly became basically (and deservedly, as I never had the commitment to do it) a punchline.

That summer became a long, slow trek to a county final, our first in twenty years. Each round, it seemed, was fixed for Tuam Stadium, at 6 p.m. on Sunday evening. That would mean no train home that evening, pints in Tuam until 2 a.m. that night, and then a semi-drunken trip to the train station on Monday morning to try and get myself right before 2 p.m. for a day's work on the radio show.

I didn't have a brilliant season on the field, in truth, but probably my best game of the year was in the county semifinal against Caltra, who had been All-Ireland club champions three years before. I kicked a point to put us ahead in injury time, we added an insurance score before the full-time whistle, and all of a sudden we were there: the county final. I was down on my haunches for twenty seconds after the final whistle, just trying to soak it all in. It was suddenly within reach.

To be a part of a small rural club reaching a senior county final is such a rare, beautiful thing. I wasn't even living there, but I could sense it every weekend when I came home. The team photos of the two previous Milltown teams that won the county championship hang in all the pubs in the village, and the thought of becoming the third team to do it was almost overwhelming.

The day of the county final itself is such an unbelievably complicated set of memories. I wasn't comfortable for the entire day, and I played terribly. The recording of the game is in my parents' house somewhere, but I couldn't ever think of watching it back. I've lived a very lucky life, one untouched so far by any real tragedy, and so I can say that it might have been the most devastating experience of my life.

I kicked two points from frees, but I barely got on the ball. After ten minutes I was wandering far from goal looking for a touch because I was nervous. After forty minutes I knew I was playing terribly.

My second pointed free came in the second half, and it was twenty-one yards out, just to the right of the posts. I took all the frees on that side, and it was as close to a gimme as you're going to get, but as I jogged over to the ball I asked our right-footed free-taker if he wanted to hit it. He looked at me almost with disgust, and I could understand why: this was my job. But I was playing so badly I was afraid I was going to miss it. In truth, I pretty much couldn't have missed it if I'd tried, but it was indicative of how frazzled my brain was. I was shying away from responsibility, and it stings me now even to think of it.

With a couple of minutes to go, I found myself underneath a high ball about twenty-five yards out from goal. In the time it took for the ball to drop to me, I had thought that I might get a chance to catch it, score a goal and undo all of the mistakes I'd made up until then. But it was not to be. The final whistle went, we were two points down, and we had to accept that we just hadn't been good enough. But my own personal failure felt even more acute.

That night in Milltown was, bizarrely, the best fun we had for that entire year. It seemed like the whole village had come back for the game, people from England and from the US, and no one who would have been out if we'd won stayed home because we'd lost. The pubs were packed ten or fifteen deep. In the midst of all the revelry, I was up ordering pints for a table full of my pals down from Dublin for the night when I caught a glimpse of one of my father's best friends sitting at the bar. This man had started crying his eyes out the night Dad told him about his Parkinson's diagnosis a few years before . . . before asking him what the hell Parkinson's was.

He had tears in his eyes again the night of the county final. He grabbed me, pulled me close and whispered, 'It would have been nice to have put that county medal in your father's hand.' No one else heard, and honestly I don't think anyone saw me crying on his shoulder either.

There was a sort of pride to be had in getting to the county final, but once we'd got there I only felt despair about my own performance. The game had been shown live on TG4, and Newstalk had become a national station a year before, and so the shame I felt at how poorly I'd played was not a particularly private one. My co-workers had made a bit of a song and dance about the point I'd kicked late on in the semi-final, but now all that was left was a kind of awkward silence. What do you say to a guy who'd blown his big chance to win a county final?

It was a joke that kept repeating itself for the following years. Anytime any of my friends mentioned the county final, they'd look at me and say: 'Too soon?'

It might still be.

*

The decision to rejoin Milltown had been vindicated. Despite the way it ended, that summer was the most emotional, the most charged experience of my football life. But we lost the management team that had done so much to get us to the final, including John Concannon, who would go on to be such a highly rated coach of Galway under Pádraic Joyce, and we drifted back to the pack. I don't know if it was just me, but even as it was happening, it always felt to me that 2007 was our one shot at glory, and we just hadn't taken it.

I continued playing, and in fact I had probably my best season of championship football the following year, but it was unsustainable. I did it for a couple more summers, and then when Newstalk got the rights to cover live games from the GAA championships, that took over my summer weekends. I tried to go back for a couple of those seasons when the live coverage was finished, in late July, but I'd missed too much football to be trying to catch up at that stage.

I was never bitter towards Milltown. I was under pressure to come home many weekends when I didn't want to, and I was under pressure in Dublin to stay home at times, but I realized it was my decision. And when I didn't want to do it any more, I stopped doing it. I know that's not the case for everyone involved in long-distance travel to play club football and hurling, and I sympathize. I hear how people my parents' age talk about fellas who head off to America for the summer, or take a year off to go travelling: those lads should understand how important they are to the club, should feel a responsibility beyond just what they want to do themselves as young people. I understand where those sentiments come from, while being resolutely on the side of any young person who wants to try and sample the world while they're still in their twenties.

As I got to thirty, it became clear that dedicating my weekends to traipsing up and down the country was out of the question. For a few years I would still throw the boots in the back of the car when I went home, and even played a couple of junior games when I was down visiting my parents, but I distinctly recall the last of those games, watching a ball fly over the bar for my only point of the game and thinking afterwards, that's probably the last point I'll ever kick in my football career.

It was a pretty depressing thought for a thirty-two-year-old to have.

That was 2014. By the time 2017 came around, there was certainly no one in Milltown waiting on me. Having served effectively six years on (self-imposed) probation, in 2017 I bit the bullet and joined Templeogue Synge Street, whose home ground was the nearest to my then home in the Liberties.

I did it for the same reason I'd joined Vincent's in 2006: I loved the game too much to just give up on it. At thirty-five years old, I felt I might have had something to offer a junior team, and Synge Street had a decent second team who were in Division 5 of Dublin adult football. (Divisions 1 and 2 are the top and bottom half of senior, Divisions 3 and 4 are intermediate, and so Division 5 was pretty much exactly the level I saw myself at.)

My friend Colm Ruane was playing with them, so I had someone to sit beside at training on the first night, and that was basically it. The welcome was warm, the football was competitive and the team was a refreshing mix of young guns, auld stagers and lads for whom the training schedule of junior football meshed nicely with their own life circumstances.

I've now played six seasons with Templeogue Synge Street,

have hosted a few fundraisers, judged a *Dancing with the Stars* competition with Mary Black (whose family are steeped in the club), and even gotten an All-Ireland final ticket or two. I feel as much of a connection with the place, with its ramshackle old pitch at Dolphin Park, and with its retired players and managers, as it's possible to feel for a club other than the one where you grew up.

For many, that's not what the GAA is about. You get one club in life and that's it. The world is refreshingly simple for those people, and maybe I envy them that. It seemed more complicated when I was not playing at all, unable to face the prospect of putting another transfer letter in to Milltown, but also unable to give up on the idea of ever playing again entirely.

Now that I'm in my forties, and very much part of the club in Templeogue Synge Street, I'm happier with my relationship with Milltown than I've perhaps ever been. It's the pure, uncomplicated love of the place I grew up in. I go back and watch our seniors play a couple of times a year. One morning in October 2021, I trained with the Templeogue Synge Street intermediates before getting in my car and driving across the country to see Milltown play St Michael's in their final championship group game.

That day, there were three possibilities for Milltown. We could seal a place in the quarter-finals with a win; we could finish clear of the relegation play-off places in the mid-table respectability of third in the case of a draw; or we could lose, finish last in the group and then face a relegation play-off.

The team that day featured no more than three men I had played senior football with. The presumption is that one's attachment to a team should weaken as one's former teammates give way to a new generation, but if anything I have found supporting Milltown even more enjoyable these last few years. Whatever leaver's guilt I may have felt even five years ago is long gone by now. Sons of former teammates have started appearing. And so it was that, on the day of the St Michael's game in 2021, I found myself roaring on young fellas I'd barely ever spoken a word to.

By the time Milltown's decisive second goal went in, I was on my feet punching the air. My former teammate Ger Bowens, then in charge of the team, could barely speak at the final whistle, he was so relieved. I was fairly drained of energy myself, and a little curious as to why I cared so much.

I hung around for a little while, bathing in the reflected glory of a three-point win, and then sat in my car for the journey home. I was in a service station later that evening, eating some Chicken McNuggets, when I thought to myself – what on earth would I say to someone who walked in and asked me what I was doing eating McNuggets in the midlands at 8 p.m. on a Sunday night on my own?

Any answer I might have given would have leaned heavily on a beautiful book I had been reading that same week called *Minor Monuments*, by Ian Maleney. He grew up outside Tullamore, in Offaly, and much of the book is about why he loves that place where he no longer lives, and about how he had to leave to properly recognize its value. There are several beautiful passages in the book on this theme, but one line in particular stood out to me: 'I have so many choices in life, but I have lost the ability to say: this is the centre of the world. Maybe this is what being local really is – the ability to say, without doubt or any subsequent clauses, this is my home.'

8. Zidanes y Pavones

After the 2007 Galway county senior football semi-final between Milltown and Caltra, we were in the bar, basking in the glory of reaching our first county final in twenty years, and the DVD of the game was put on to ensure the night stayed well lubricated.

We were all feeling on top of the world, because we knew it had been the sort of solid team performance that we had all contributed to. And then we watched the game again, and one thing became very clear: our two county players, Diarmaid Blake and Darren Mullahy, were the reason we were in the county final.

Michael Meehan had scored two early goals for Caltra before Darren moved to full-back and snuffed him out completely. When our wing-backs went forward, Diarmaid was always on their shoulder. He caught his fair share of kick-outs and took most of the frees in our half. The two of them set up scores when they went forward themselves. Between them, they must have touched the ball a hundred times.

We were all equal, but some were more equal than others. We had a few lads who had played for Galway at minor and under-21 level, and John Devane had played senior for Galway for a couple of years before that as well, but that season Diarmaid and Darren were a class apart. We all leaned on them massively, looked to them for leadership, and took our cues from them, regardless of where we were on the pitch. Our success that year was a classic case of a good club team being elevated by top-quality county players.

As GAA club players we can roar on our county team on any given Sunday, and then, the very next week, we line out with those same players in club games. Of course, players in other sports operate on multiple levels – toggling between an international team and a club. But the GAA, being an amateur mass-participation organization with a huge number of clubs, is different. If GAA was like soccer or rugby, the very best players would cluster together at a small number of top clubs. Instead, GAA inter-county stars play – with rare exceptions – for the club they were born into, alongside teammates who may be at a dramatically lower level of skill.

Diarmaid and Darren were the best Milltown footballers of the last thirty years, and two of the best club players in Galway this century. I was lucky to play with them throughout my football career, starting at the age of five. When we were teenagers, just starting out playing senior football, Galway were on top of the football world. They won the All-Ireland in 1998, lost the final in 2000 after a replay, and won again in 2001. I played multiple times against nearly all of the members of that team, and every one of those games meant something to them.

By way of contrast, I once played nine holes at Seapoint Golf Club with Darren Clarke at a sponsorship event, around the time he won the British Open. I can certainly say that I played a few holes with one of the best golfers in the world, but the experience had about as much to do with going down the eighteenth in contention for a major as my weekly drive to Lidl has to do with the Monaco Grand Prix.

By contrast, when I played against teams that had Ja Fallon, or Kevin Walsh, or Seán Óg de Paor playing, those boys were competing for real. There was no one on that Galway

1998 team that phoned it in for their clubs. When they lined out, in league or in championship, they were prepared to lead.

Michael Donnellan was extraordinary to watch playing club football: just pure poetry in motion. And he was so likeable, so beloved by everyone. One of his Dunmore teammates once booted me across the ankle in a game in Milltown when I was barely out of secondary school. As I lay on the ground in tears, certain my ankle had been broken (it hadn't), Michael came over and started whispering in my ear, saying what a bad tackle it was. He even shouldered me off the field. I was in so much pain it barely registered at the time, but in A&E later that evening I wasn't thinking about his teammate, but wondering how I could get word to Michael to tell him how much I appreciated it.

On another occasion we played Moycullen in a league game and I found myself playing centre-forward, up against Paul Clancy. He was another unfailingly polite young man, and engaged me in conversation about my journalism career, what I'd studied in college, how Milltown were going that year . . . all while absolutely cleaning me out. It was the most low-key emasculating hour of my life. His domination of me was so complete, and so effortless, that I couldn't even feel frustrated by it.

In those instances, I was dealing with two of life's easier-going characters in Clancy and Donnellan. There were others, and Pádraic Joyce was foremost among this cohort, who were intent on dominating every physical encounter, every confrontation, every chat to the officials. Joyce was a big personality, a national name, and he knew how to wield that power in ways both big and small. It was there in how he spoke to the ref, but also in the contempt with which he handled anyone trying to rough him up physically. There was no ruffling him, no getting under his skin. He made you feel foolish for even trying it. Kevin Walsh had a similar temperament – and maybe it's no surprise that each of them went on to manage his county.

Joyce was a force of nature. It's a badge of honour to say that you won't ever be intimidated on a football field, but there's no doubt Joyce intimidated club players. He intimidated me, for sure. Here was a man who had scored ten points in an All-Ireland final when the game was there to be won, and who cared more about his club than you did about yours. If you doubted the latter, just ask him and he'd give you your answer.

The story is well told about him captaining the Ireland International Rules team to victory, and showing up in Carna in north Connemara the following morning to play a league game with Killererin. That level of dedication was there every single time he played for his club. He exuded authority. When I read John Updike's famous *New Yorker* piece about the great Ted Williams's last home game with the Boston Red Sox – in which he writes that Williams 'radiated, from afar, the hard blue glow of high purpose' – I thought immediately of Joyce. He demanded high standards from his teammates, he demanded protection from referees, and he took zero shit from anyone.

He was the central character in every game he played, and he welcomed that burden. That Galway team had a few generational talents, but you won't find anyone who would say that any other man on that team came close to Pádraic Joyce as a club player. He was genuinely mindbogglingly good for fifteen years with Killererin.

Even when he wasn't playing, he exerted a gravitational pull among club players of his generation. There have always been at least seven or eight senior club teams in Galway within fifteen miles of Tuam, sometimes more, so it would stand to reason that there would often be four or five senior championship games played in Tuam Stadium every championship weekend. If you weren't playing until the Sunday evening, you might head into the Saturday double-header, just for something to do. If you were one half of a double bill, you'd often see at least a half of the game before you or the game after you.

So without even really trying you'd watch a ton of football every weekend, often with players from other teams milling around and chatting. And the giant figure at the centre of that broad circle was, of course, Joyce. He loved football so much, and lived for it so completely, that he was barely ever a dispassionate viewer. And if players made mistakes, he could be devastatingly cutting. I never thought he rated me much as a player, but at least I knew that I was far from alone.

(Diarmaid, our county man, was another who couldn't help voicing his opinion at these games. My brother was once sitting beside him at a Caltra game, soon after the six Meehan brothers had been so central in winning them the 2004 All-Ireland club final. Outside the Meehan galácticos, the standard of player was a bit more inconsistent, which led Diarmaid to shout out at the top of his voice in Tuam Stadium one day in the general direction of one of the less-decorated members of that team who was dithering in possession – 'Ah lad, just pass it to a Meehan!')

The frustration that Joyce felt watching in the stand was obviously magnified a hundred times when he was out on the field with his clubmates, and he could fairly cut them down to size as well. But his authority was unquestioned. He wasn't just the best player, he was the best clubman. And he dragged Killererin, kicking and screaming, to four county titles. Not all inter-county players are capable of that. In fact, the list is vanishingly small.

My Templeogue Synge Street clubmate and erstwhile coach Adrian O'Flynn spent a number of years on the fringes of the Leitrim team before finally breaking into the league side one spring. When his county manager decided to rotate him out of the squad for a game against Kilkenny they were expected to win easily, he was told to go play a challenge game for his club. He was in the form of his life, and he turned up playing at centre-back and expecting to stroll through this challenge game – bestride it like a colossus and leave the watching public agog at his mastery of the finer arts of the sport.

He got his first ball close to the sideline, decided to contemptuously sidestep his opponent . . . and lost the ball in contact. 'OK, don't know what happened there, no problem.' He got onto his next ball, saw a gap through which he could drive a defence-splitting pass . . . and drilled it straight to an opponent. One of his own teammates gave him a bit of an earful, nothing too insulting, basically trying to gee him up a bit – 'Alright, Aido, let's go now.' And of course Adrian's reaction to this was to immediately question what he was doing wasting his time at this club challenge game.

And so he was trying, but he was also sulking a little bit at the injustice of having to play this game when he was a county man. And then he sat in his car after the game, and realized that sulking was just a way of protecting his own ego. He thought about his teammate who had been the only man from their club playing inter-county for the past ten years, a man he thought had been acting the bollocks for that entire time.

And he realized – 'OK, that's what he's been putting up with for the last decade. It's no wonder he looks depressed coming back to us.'

That was his only year playing regularly for his county team. Conversely, he was in no doubt that the best football he played for his club was when he was on the bench for the county team for the entire year. He was fit, he was lightly played, he was hungry. When he was getting into the inter-county team, his form for his club dipped.

The most influential hurler in the country at the moment, Limerick's Gearóid Hegarty, plays for a junior club. He drives the standards in the best hurling team in the country, and then he is supposed to acclimatize seamlessly to a club scene where, as Hegarty said a few weeks after the 2022 All-Ireland final, the sliotars were still drenched wet from the previous game and the grass of their home pitch was six inches long.

Similarly, we all marvelled at David Clifford's time playing junior football for Fossa, which culminated in an All-Ireland club title for them in early 2023. And while many of us club players found ourselves wondering just how much fun it would be to play alongside possibly the best ever to do it at that level, there was also an understanding that it can't have been all that easy for Clifford. He referred to it himself – the pressure on him to perform, when he obviously knew that pressure couldn't be spread around as evenly as it is with the Kerry seniors. His teammates didn't need to see Clifford down training with them on a Tuesday night if he just didn't fancy it for any reason. But that freedom comes with the price of being asked to win games almost single-handedly time after time after time.

It can be trickier for high-level senior clubs that depend massively on their county players. A friend of mine who played senior inter-county football spoke about finding himself in 'Zidane mode' at various times in his club career. This, as he described it to me, is where inter-county footballers come back to their clubs thinking that they can get by purely on their technical superiority over the players they're playing against. They swan around, possibly bearing the Gallic countenance that gives this attitude its name, thinking that they will be allowed to dictate the terms of the game just by dint of their reputation. Zizou might have been able to get away with running World Cup quarter-finals while looking like he could be wearing slippers and smoking a pipe, but not many others can.

You will see examples of this in every county championship. But the reality is that Gaelic football does not really lend itself to that sort of attitude, particularly if you're a county player that your teammates are hoping will really influence the game where it matters most. No matter how wide the gulf in skill between a county player and the players on the opposition, the superior player will still always be given a stern examination – either physically or mentally. You're going to be singled out for treatment, by fair means or foul, and if you're not willing to get stuck in, no amount of ethereal movement is going to cut it.

A more sympathetic reading of that is that the psychological calmness required to play in front of 80,000 people asks county players to basically trick themselves into staying cool under pressure. You're asking your body to tell itself it's calm, when every external factor is roaring the exact opposite. And then when you're playing in front of eighty people at a club game, the question is almost completely reversed.

Instead of asking, 'Can I do this? Is this overwhelming?' the question becomes, 'What am I doing here? Where is my motivation for this?'

County players know that the focus is on them all the time. They are inevitably going to be frustrated at having to play with players who are not as talented as they are. But the merest suggestion of that frustration showing will make you look bad, and make the team look bad.

There is a significant upside to playing club football, of course. Provided it's handled proactively by clubs and club managers, you can be reintegrated swiftly and not feel isolated and under pressure – 'an interloper in your own club', as it was once described to me. After spending six months with your county team, playing for your club is the easiest possible way for you to connect back not just with the people you played with as a kid, but also with the simple, visceral, almost childlike experience of playing for enjoyment's sake.

There's no need to be at the pitch an hour or more before training is due to begin, for a start. This is a relatively recent development that has apparently become ingrained at inter-county level, and is something I'm going to go ahead and blame Stephen Cluxton for. According to legend, he was the first man in to Dublin training every night for a large part of his career, and if your captain is there an hour or ninety minutes before training begins, after a while it starts to put the focus on other players. Slowly, Dublin players started arriving earlier and earlier for training. And the more Dublin won, the more their every nuance was inspected, to see if it could help other teams. Before you knew it, county players all over the country were arriving an hour before training. They might be getting some kicking practice in, some pre-hab work, or some video analysis. It might sound like a high-performance environment to some people, but to me it just sounds exhausting.

With your club, you can show up five minutes before the session is due to start, dominate and drive standards in training routines and games, and then head straight home again. Your mere presence indicates how seriously you're taking it. Clubs want their inter-county players to dominate in games, and they're happy to let their stars figure out how best to ensure that happens. If you need a rest from training, take a rest. If you need a holiday after the county season is over, go for it. The equation remains the same.

When the pressure comes on, we're going to be looking at you. And while that has its downsides, you're an inter-county player for a reason – you're better than everyone else. Getting a chance to show it, in front of your neighbours and your peers, has still got to be a thrill.

9. Town and Country

I have a permanent reminder of my first ever game of adult football. My smile was by no means one for Hollywood even before I played Junior A Championship, but there's a tooth right in front that is slightly discoloured as a result of what I would term a reasonably legitimate belt in the face from the Corofin full-back as I went up to field a high ball in Tuam Stadium that afternoon in 1999.

He was a lovely fella, everyone assured me, but it wasn't a whole pile of fun for me for the next few days, as I watched a pale blue discolouration creep up from the bottom of my tooth to my gumline. I went to the dentist in Tuam to see if there was anything that could be done. 'No, you're grand, it'll just slowly die and probably stay roughly the same colour as it is now,' he told me. And that was that.

I was sixteen, but I was already six foot two or three and more than ready to play at that level. And even so, my development was slower than I wanted it to be, because a lad my age – Diarmaid Blake – had already played against Tuam Stars in the Senior Football Championship a few weeks earlier. Diarmaid even ended up winning Man of the Match in a losing effort, up against grown men, four full months shy of his seventeenth birthday.

At the time, I thought it was an extraordinary thing for Diarmaid to make that step-up so quickly. But when I looked recently at Milltown teams from the following years, I saw that three more players did the exact same thing in the next three seasons: played senior championship football in the year that they turned seventeen.

They were all exceptional players, and would all go on to win All-Ireland medals at under-21 level for Galway in either 2002 or 2005, but the fast-tracking of teenagers into senior football was the norm for clubs our size. We were in no position to wait patiently for our best young players to develop.

If I thought I was a good footballer, then playing senior club football as a teenager was non-negotiable. I wanted to be a part of it, as quickly as I could. We had won our fair share of games at underage, and everyone in my age group knew that the club was looking to us to inject something into a senior team that wasn't winning games. We wanted to help, the club needed us to step up, and we were impatient to get started. As far as we were concerned, Diarmaid would be the first of us to play senior football, but he would by no means be the last.

Everything is different now. If those players were coming through today, Milltown would not be allowed to play them at any adult level (senior, intermediate or junior) before 1 January in the year that they turned eighteen.

Evan Ferguson played professional soccer for Bohemians in the League of Ireland Premier Division at fourteen. If he'd decided to play GAA, he'd have had to wait three and a half more years before he was even allowed to play for his home club of St Colmcille's in Bettystown, County Meath, let alone for his county. He had scored against Arsenal in the Premier League, and been capped by his country, at an age when he would not have been allowed to play for the St Colmcille's Junior As.

Well-informed people tell me that the GAA changed the age rule out of a desire to avoid situations where a championship run by a county's minor team caused the postponement of senior club fixtures in that county. In other words, adult players could lose a summer of football because their clubs were often quite dependent on teenagers who also played minor inter-county. That problem no longer exists, because of the subsequent decoupling of the inter-county and club seasons. But up until the introduction of the split season, it was a real problem.

In 2007, the year I played in the Galway county final for Milltown, the county championship was repeatedly delayed because the Galway minor team were on a march to the All-Ireland final, which they ended up winning. I don't remember watching that game, and maybe the fact that this brilliant young team of footballers had denied me a regular stream of matches that summer had something to do with that informal boycott. That sort of fixture clash doesn't happen any more, but the higher age threshold for playing senior remains. And while it might have saved my footballing summer in 2007 if it had been in force back then, I'm not sure I like it.

The higher age threshold for playing senior allowed the GAA to change the minor grade from under-18, which it had been for some ninety years, to under-17. At the inter-county level, the changes saved seventeen-year-olds from what used to be a pile-up of commitments: club minor, under-21 and senior, schools football and/or hurling, or third-level GAA. The thinking was that under-17s would play only with their own age group, which would allow them to focus on the Leaving Cert when they were eighteen.

Viewed through that prism, it has been a success. The move to under-17 has protected our best young players. But here we see an example of a rule for the top level of the sport having repercussions all the way down to the smallest unit of the GAA. At this level, the reaction to the changes has been volcanic. Clubs teetering on the edge of extinction are denied the chance to pick young players who are physically and mentally ready for the challenge of playing adult football. If you're Valentia Young Islanders, in south Kerry, and you have a couple of good seventeen-year-olds, their availability, or non-availability, according to the rule book, could be the difference between fielding a side and not fielding a side in any given year.

If those seventeen-year-olds on Valentia Island are anything like me and my contemporaries at that age in Milltown, they probably can't wait for the opportunity to play adult football. And the smaller the club, the more intimately connected the juvenile and adult sections invariably are.

I remember standing in front of a group of Templeogue Synge Street under-13s a couple of years ago and telling them that my relationship with the GAA has been one of the most fulfilling parts of my adult life, and that a lifelong relationship with a club, whether as a player, a coach or an administrator, is a gift that you will reap the benefits of for the rest of your life.

But the club can have only so many volunteers, and so many players. A lot of clubs in Dublin are gigantic, but they are such effective harvesters of young people that 60 or 70 per cent of them won't have a direct relationship with the GAA club beyond their seventeenth birthday. They can't – there's just no room for them. When those clubs see a drop off in participation after minor level, they must secretly breathe a sigh of relief. Many urban and large town clubs have as many minor teams as they have adult teams, which very succinctly illustrates why they're happy to let 50 per cent or more of their players drift away from the club altogether once they hit adulthood.

When I was talking to those under-13s, I was perhaps guilty of bringing my experiences of a small rural club to a city club with a rather different demographic. The more I consider my experiences in both of my clubs, the more I see the issue of player retention in each as being rather like the difference between 'opt-in' and 'opt-out' schemes for organ donation.

With Milltown, you basically have to choose to stop being involved in the club. The progression from Go Games, with no winners or losers, to minor to junior and, if you're good enough, to senior, is there for everyone. If you opt out, you opt out, but if you're willing to play adult football at eighteen, there will be a place for you. And, critically, many of your new teammates at adult level will be family members, or your neighbours, or your older brothers' or sisters' best friends.

For city clubs, it's the opposite – you have to opt in. When you finish up your juvenile career, you will barely even know every player at your own age-grade, if they've been spread out over three or four teams. As an eighteen-year-old, you will find the next step in your football or hurling career is into an adult dressing room where you might not know a single person. In fact, many urban clubs are so big that the juvenile and adult sections can feel like two totally different entities. When Templeogue Synge Street organizes events to bring those two parts of the club together, they know how high the stakes are. Rather than worrying about losing half their players once they 'age out' of juvenile football, it's a wonder they can hold on to the ones they manage to keep.

In 2021, Templeogue Synge Street had four minor football

teams. What happens to those seventy-odd lads once the year is over? The very best players will get moved on to the senior and intermediate panels. The ones with potential, but who might need a couple more years of physical development, go to the junior sides, alongside those for whom the game is simply something to be enjoyed. So even the young players who stick around will more than likely be separated from many of their peers.

If the club can hold on to a seventeen-year-old for even two more years, then we'll probably have that player for life. Some young people will finish their minor football careers, and consign the GAA to a wardrobe full of other things that they also used to do when they were a kid, and move on without a moment's pause. But the ones who keep coming back at eighteen, nineteen and twenty will more than likely stick around for a lot longer than that.

For Milltown, the problem is the complete opposite. At the moment, Milltown's underage teams compete in the county's lower divisions, often against bigger clubs' second and third teams, and they struggle for numbers. The standard of football will be low, our best players will be developing bad habits, and losing at that level can be extremely disheartening.

If you want to look at the teams dominating underage football and hurling in Galway, draw a ring of about twenty-five kilometres around Galway city. The clubs inside that ring are thriving. I have two brothers who live in Athenry and another who lives in Oranmore. Those clubs are stretched to the limit to provide games for everyone who wants to play, similar in many respects to Templeogue Synge Street.

Beyond that ring around the city, in Milltown and other rural clubs, there just aren't enough underage players. And yet, Milltown's senior team competes in the top division and is highly competitive. Milltown has been remarkably efficient at developing and retaining promising underage players into adulthood.

When I'm at home in Milltown, engaged in conversation about the future of the club, I'll ask about the demographics, about the numbers in our national schools, and our lack of underage success. I will be told in no uncertain terms that 'we're fucked'. I've been hearing this for eight or nine years now. And each year I go home to watch our senior team out-perform expectations and defy odds and generally behave as if our position in Galway football is non-negotiable.

Milltown celebrated sixty straight years as a senior club in Galway in 2022. Only Tuam Stars have retained their senior status for longer in the entire county. It's an extraordinary run – an achievement as special in its way as the two county titles we've won. Of course, that's not to say that gravity won't, eventually, make itself felt.

But in December 2020 I was able to watch a Galway team with Milltown's Eoin Mannion and Jack Kirrane on the pitch in Croke Park as the final whistle went, beating a Dublin team with Lorcan O'Dell of Templeogue Synge Street on board, in the All-Ireland under-20 final. Their clubs gave them very different routes to that final, but all three of them got there eventually. The two lads from Milltown are best buddies with my cousin Niall, and I've shared a dressing room with Lorcan. In that scenario, you hope Lorcan plays brilliantly, but Galway win . . . and, as has almost always been the case in his fine young career to date, Lorcan held up his end of the bargain, and Galway did the rest.

There are clubs, like Oranmore-Maree and Claregalway, that have huge numbers at underage level but have nevertheless spent time in the Intermediate Football Championship in recent years. Such clubs' second teams regularly come down to Milltown and beat us in underage football. But we've found a way to take one or two players from our underage teams every year, get them into a senior team, and make them competitive. It's getting harder and harder, but it's still happening.

At underage levels, one option for Milltown and other clubs that struggle for numbers is to amalgamate with neighbouring clubs. The standard at which the amalgamated team is playing will rise, and the desperate scramble for players will no longer be necessary. On the other hand, something precious is lost. The jersey will change, the name will change, and the history of both clubs will be diluted somehow. Milltown are fighting the good fight so far, and my impression is that amalgamation is not something anyone is ready to countenance . . . yet.

The situation in Dublin couldn't be more different. A far lower percentage of underage players continue seamlessly into the adult teams. But sometimes people come back after long absences. Every January since I joined Templeogue Synge Street, a couple of lads I've never seen before have joined training. I hear the chatter: 'This guy's a genius . . . That guy played minor football for Dublin . . . This guy played senior championship for us five years ago.' The churn of players is bewildering.

And there is, of course, another question: Why on earth should the development of one of those young footballers, just out of minor, be halted by the presence on the club's second adult team of an ageing, borderline immobile blow-in such as your correspondent here? This is a key dilemma, and one which I am wrestling with more and more as I get closer to the inevitable end of my playing days. I could tell you right now the name of the talented young player whose career I'm holding up, and I feel I've a responsibility to take that into account every year when I decide if I'm going to continue playing, and at what level.

I have a personal desire, born out of whatever competitive spirit that remains in my forties, to see if I can still perform at a certain level. That's an important driver in any decision I make. But I also have to think about the wider responsibility. I've played for six years for the club's second team – a valuable proving ground for any young player before he takes the next step and becomes a senior footballer. How much longer should I stand in the way of that progression? And even if a manager thinks I can do a job at that level, should I take that decision out of his hands? I'm not just a player for the club: I'm a member. I need to be mindful of the club's best interests and of the next stages of my involvement – be that as a coach, or an administrator, or even just as an engaged and committed fan.

It's a source of wonder to me that I've been able to join a club in Dublin in my mid-thirties and make deep connections that will hopefully remain long after I'm finished playing. The welcome that so many of us have received is a gift that country people living in Dublin sometimes take for granted. Equally, so many clubs in Dublin have benefited from the contributions of country people who, once they finished playing, threw themselves into the job of building, sustaining, and growing clubs. It's no surprise to see how many clubs chart their development back to a group of countrymen who moved into an area for work in the 1950s and 60s, and set about making a GAA club to call their own.

*

Clubs find a way to make the system work, but there is no doubt that there are too many of them in the country, and too few in urban areas. It's a Dublin problem, but it's also a problem in medium-sized towns where there's only one club and far too many kids to cater for.

Take the example of Naas, a big town (over 21,000 people) with a high proportion of young families – and only one GAA club. The population of Naas has nearly doubled in the last thirty years. In 1990, when it won the Kildare county football final, the town may not have seemed out of the ordinary in having only one club. As its population increased, the club's primary concern would have been to provide a structure for the GAA to develop and grow in the town, in line with demand: more teams, more pitches.

Their results on the field certainly didn't suggest a behemoth: they went thirty-one years without adding to that 1990 county football title. But in 2021 they ended that drought, and won a third county hurling title in a row for good measure. They did a double in 2022 as well.

During the years when Naas grappled with the town's population doubling in size in a generation, without any on-field senior success, it would have been difficult indeed to argue that Naas needed another GAA club. Now that they have started winning all around them, while clubs in rural Kildare struggle to compete, the idea of forming another club to increase participation levels in the town might feel like punishment for too much success. It's a fiendishly hard needle to thread.

'One parish, one club' is a slogan you sometimes hear in the GAA, but it's not a rule. Some mid-sized towns, and even some small parishes, have ended up with more than one club – usually as a result of local rows and family feuds in places where, as Brendan Behan observed of the republican movement, 'the first item on the agenda is the split'. But waiting on people to fall out with each other is a shaky basis for a national strategy, so it looks like the GAA may have to be a little more proactive than that. Demographers expect the urbanization of Ireland to continue over the coming decades. Country clubs will continue to get smaller, while the urban clubs get ever bigger.

The GAA has been attempting to grasp this nettle for a long time. When its Community Development, Urban and Rural Committee delivered its report in 2021, it referenced the work of *nine* previous committees that had tried to do what they themselves were attempting: to map out the effects of the rural-to-urban migration of the last forty years. The fact that there have been ten such committees, but no noteworthy actions, suggests that the GAA sees itself as being unable to adjust to economic and demographic change.

There may also be limits to people's appetite for such adjustments. For many communities, the GAA club is the last thing standing after the Garda station, the post office, and the local pub have all gone. To underestimate how jealously rural villages will guard their own club would be foolish indeed, because country clubs taking on the 'townies' is a tale as old as the GAA itself.

Faced with disparities in population, rural clubs cling to certain ideas. They reckon that, no matter how many young players a town or city club produces, they can still only play fifteen of them at a time when it comes to the crunch at senior level. Rural clubs also believe that, when push comes to shove, they'll just care more than the townies. That the honour of the little village counts for more than a vast, sprawling network of housing estates in an urban setting. My father was friendly with enough people from urban clubs to realize that when they said Milltown was a tough place to come and get a result, they really bloody meant it.

One of them, a hugely respected figure in third-level GAA, told him once that Milltown had a (strangely specific) four-point advantage on the city club he was affiliated with every time they played, just because we were more united and more determined than any club from an urban area could ever be. I don't know if that's true, but I do know I believed it to be true when I was a player with Milltown, which is almost the same thing, isn't it?

After I had put in a couple of good years with Templeogue Synge Street, there was a part of me that would've loved the chance to play with Milltown one more time. And the idea that I wouldn't be able to play intermediate in one county and senior (or more likely junior!) in a different county, when it's impossible for the two teams ever to meet each other, raises the question of why you're not allowed to play for two teams in two different counties simultaneously.

It might be useful to clubs smaller than Milltown, with exiled players a lot better than me, and it would take the emotional blackmail element out of having to make a decision. Of course, some clubs would be OK with allowing one of their players to play league games with a different club in a different county, and others wouldn't. That would be their own decision to make. But for some clubs the availability of one or two lads living and playing in another county could be the difference between life and death. And that's something worth considering.

*

I often think about the next ten or twenty years, after I'm finished as a player. I don't have kids, and never will, so I won't naturally be drawn back to Templeogue Synge Street as a parent. What does it mean to be a 'blow-in' (said with love!) in a club you're no longer playing for?

There was a brief attempt to second me onto the executive a couple of years ago, which I expertly wriggled away from, but maybe a career in club administration lies ahead for me. Or management? There have been times in recent years when some training session talks were handed over to me, but I don't think I've the decisiveness for it.

So if both those avenues are closed, what's it to be? I know what brings me back to Milltown games as an ex-player, and I hope I've put down enough roots to ensure I'm equally welcome back at Synger games as a member and supporter when I've finally hung up the boots. A lifelong connection wasn't what I was looking for when I wandered up to Dolphin Park, but it's what I want now.

10. The Pitch

On May 19th 1900, 'great crowds travelled on wheels, horse-back and on foot to witness a red-letter in football on the pitch at Gurranes Racecourse outside Tuam'. This was for a tournament in which Milltown John O'Keane's participated, unfortunately losing to Tuam Stars by two points to nil. In descriptions of the play mention is made of the valiant efforts of Milltown players Flaherty, Reddington, Mullarkey, Slattery, Gilmore and Killoyne, but the reporter 'Sport' also wrote – 'The Stars were beaten a few Sundays ago by this same O'Keane's team, but then the Milltown field which they played in was only fit for mountain sheep or goats to gambol in, and certainly not fit or suitable for a game of football.'

– *Tuam News* report quoted by Jim Carney,
'Milltown '81', a souvenir publication to mark
Milltown GAA club's victory in the 1981
County Galway Senior Football Championship

On behalf of Milltown G.A.A. Club, it is my honour and privilege to welcome everyone to the Blessing and Official Opening of our new park.

For our club it is the culmination of 10 years' hard work in the development of this important parish amenity. A decade of mostly voluntary development work, and major fund-raising, to which there was a most generous response, has borne fruit today, and to everybody who played a part, big or small, in turning the old parish football field into such a splendid park, with its very fine dressing-room facilities, I say a sincere Thank You, with a very special *buíochas* to those wonderful Milltown people overseas who did not forget us either, just as we do not forget them.

Cead míle fáilte also, to the stars of Milltown teams down through the years, also here today, and to friendly rivals and neighbours Galway and Mayo. But the main toast is to the loyalty and unwavering commitment which has kept Milltown football alive and vibrant, at underage and adult level. Today is the supreme manifestation of parish pride in the Blue jersey.

– Club chairman Tom McManus, writing in the
programme for the official opening of the new
Milltown GAA club home grounds, 26 August 1990

There is a picture hanging on my wall of the GAA pitch on Inishturk, an island off the coast of Mayo. It was taken by a photographer called Paul Carroll, who has compiled one of the most interesting GAA books of recent decades – *Gaelic Fields*. For seven years, Carroll went around the country taking photographs of matches at GAA grounds. Bucolic rural settings, sweeping seaside vistas, inner-city pitches fashioned through toil and endeavour, that age-old fight for a patch of grass amidst the concrete. With each photo there is no information given other than the location, the two teams involved, and the final score. There is no indication of the relative importance of the game in question, or the standard, or the age-grade. It's all about the place – how the GAA club fits into the landscape and makes itself integral.

The pitch in Inishturk is, suffice to say, not normal. It

looks to be maybe half the size of a regular pitch, the teams appear to be playing eleven-a-side, if that, and in the foreground, as a narrow gravel path sweeps down towards the pitch, there are two horses. Sheep graze the hills surrounding the pitch, which is set between rocky abutments and steep fields of thin grass. Beyond that is the Atlantic Ocean, and even further back, Inishbofin and Connemara in the distance.

The final score was Inishturk Island 0-9, Clare Island 0-8 . . . and, even though we aren't told if this was a game officially sanctioned by the Mayo county board, or part of the All-Island GAA Championship (a part of GAA life worth a book on its own, surely), or simply a challenge game between the two, I think we can presume the rivalry is keenly contested.

The book is full of such revelations. Sometimes the play is front and centre, other times the eye is drawn to what lies beyond the field. The church and the big house (possibly the priest's?) overlooking the pitch in Cootehill; the Odlums factory in Portarlington; the Harland and Wolff shipyards from a vantage point in West Belfast.

The idea of the book was emphatically not to take photographs of only the most beautiful GAA grounds in the country, although there are a number of images that would certainly fulfil that criterion. The book attempts to show what 'the pitch', as so many are called by those who use them, means in communities.

The club in Milltown is at the north end of the village, so no one needs too many directions to find it. Its grounds and facilities have been improved and extended constantly over the past fifty years. As you enter, the playing field is twelve feet or more below you, spread out in front of you to your right. The near sideline and the parking spaces behind the goal closest to you form two natural embankments – ideal places to park your car, and watch the game from the driver's seat when the weather gets particularly inclement.

When I was growing up, the built amenities consisted of only two dressing rooms, but an extension has added two more dressing rooms and a small gym, and an extension on the other side of the building contains a kitchen and committee room. There's a small AstroTurf pitch and ball wall in a pen beside the dressing rooms.

On the other side of the main pitch there's a stand that can seat 200 people, and behind the other goal, furthest from the entrance, is a small training area going right down to the banks of the River Clare, which runs parallel to that pitch and all the way through north-east Galway and into Lough Corrib.

The river is hidden from view by a stand of conifers. The only time I ever even thought about the river and its proximity to the pitch was in the middle of the summer of 2010, after a particularly intense training session, when we decided we'd wade into the water to cool down afterwards. It was a beautiful day, there was the usual post-training endorphin rush among us all, and we were able to see the village in a whole new light, from a vantage point I'd never experienced.

As we looked back upstream, we could see the bridge in the middle of the village, the church, Sheridan's at the top of the hill, and two more riverside pubs on the south bank. It was gorgeous. I think it was the moment I convinced myself we were going to win the county title that year, in fact. I could see myself waxing lyrical about it to an *Irish Times* journalist over a coffee as we prepared to face the Sligo champions in the first round of the Connacht Club Championship, still basking in the glow of winning the county. 'That was the day, Malachy – the day it all came together for us. That was the day we realized what we were playing for.' Suffice to say, the county title, and the *Irish Times* interview, never happened.

There's a second full-size training pitch behind the stand, which means the main pitch can be kept in perfect condition. In a parish with barely 1,500 inhabitants, it's an incredibly impressive, spacious, comfortable set-up.

The scale of fundraising that goes on is a minor miracle in communities of Milltown's size. I spoke to a friend of mine who works with charities devising their donation campaigns, and who has also been leaned upon by various GAA clubs to help guide their fundraising. Unbelievably, for the vast majority of GAA clubs, the problem is not about setting goals or reaching targets. The targets are always achieved eventually. By hook or by crook, the community will step up. The bank will look favourably. The bills will get paid. But a good fundraising model is about getting a range of people to donate, not relying on the same few individuals or businesses every time. And, conversely, not being able to raise the money for a major development also means that the best people in your club are stressed out and focused solely on trying to pay for it. Their time and effort is a cost to the club too.

Fundraising goes hand-in-hand with what the club can get from other sources – be that the local or county council, the Leader fund, or the GAA centrally. These are often small amounts, useful when embarking on new projects in distinct phases, as happened in Milltown. The other major source of funding is the government's Sports Capital Programme, a uniquely competitive environment in which clubs all over the country jostle for grants.

In my view, the state ought to require clubs in receipt of these grants to share their facilities with other local sports clubs. If you get a government grant then it should come with some facility to ensure that the whole community benefits, not just the GAA club.

One obstacle to this is the GAA's rule book. Rule 5.1 states that 'all property including grounds, clubhouses, halls, dressing rooms and handball alleys owned or controlled by units of the GAA shall be used only for the purpose of or in connection with the playing of the games controlled by the GAA and for other purposes in accordance with the aims of the GAA, that may be sanctioned by Central Council'.

There was a high-profile incident in late 2021 when Ballygunner in Waterford, one of the most successful hurling clubs in Ireland during the 2010s, was found to have been renting out their indoor facilities to Bohemian FC's academy. This was an arrangement that both Ballygunner and Bohemians were delighted with. Bohemians had a chance for their young kids to train and play indoors in the depths of winter, and Ballygunner were accruing rental fees from the use of their hall. An anonymous whistle-blower (really!) made a complaint to Croke Park, and the GAA felt forced to act. Ballygunner missed out on valuable rent and Bohemians were left to put their kids back out in the rain.

Rule 5.1 is routinely and unapologetically broken in clubs up and down the country. To enforce it would be to cut off revenue streams from other local clubs (or from lads who just want to play five-a-side on a Monday night), as well as creating ill-will between the GAA club and teams in other codes.

At a local level, it is counter-productive to the entire idea of promoting sport if community projects can be exclusively ring-fenced by specific clubs. And that goes for soccer and rugby and other sports clubs in receipt of funding too, of course. The government could make it a legal requirement, but the GAA should also be proactive. Rule 5.1 should go.

In Milltown, there is no soccer or rugby club, so that issue doesn't really arise. Since 1998 there's been an LGFA club in the village, and even though we don't yet operate the 'one club' model, they're an integral part of Milltown GAA, in the lived sense of that term, and have full use of the facilities.

When the inevitable happens, and the LGFA, the Camogie Association and the GAA are fully and formally merged, more GAA clubs will be able to form closer bonds with their female counterparts. The two main issues in any community in relation to the different organizations are fundraising and access to playing fields. Joint fundraising initiatives have taken place already in Milltown and, while access to facilities hasn't been sorted out overnight, and there was certainly a wariness about access to the main pitch in the early days, the prospect of alienating half the parish very quickly came to seem self-defeating. So the grounds stand as a monument to the hard work of pretty much the entire community. Why wouldn't we be proud of it?

GAA clubs are obsessed with their grounds. It's as clear an indication of the Irish fixation on land ownership as any number of articles about house prices. More often than not, your home ground places you directly in the centre of your community. It anchors you in it, establishes you as one of the cornerstones of the village, along with the church and the pub. When I see tiny clubs with beautifully appointed grounds, in areas otherwise not exactly overburdened with infrastructure, I can't help but be reminded of those fifteenth-century French Catholic towns where they built beautiful cathedrals while the townspeople ate their own dogs.

For Templeogue Synge Street, my club in Dublin, the situation is rather different. Our pitches are located just off the Crumlin Road in Dolphin's Barn, which in itself can be a little confusing. Synge Street is in Dublin 8, Templeogue is Dublin 6. The two GAA clubs merged in 1999, and our home ground is in Dublin 12.

The dressing rooms are cold, draughty and inhospitable. One of the two pitches is bumpy and uneven. Repeated attempts to redevelop and improve the facilities have failed, due to wrangling too internecine and tedious to go into here, but ambitious plans are now in place to give the club the home it deserves. As the club embarks on a fundraising drive that has to take into account soaring building costs and the scarcity of available green spaces in Dublin, we will have to think carefully about how we raise the money. But there is a recognition that, regardless of other revenue streams, our members will have to step up – that for it to really mean something to everyone, we'll all have to contribute what we can. It is crucial that club members view their contributions as more than a simple transaction. Your direct debit, or your one-off payment, buys you an emotional stake in the club.

There is also the inconvenient truth that our rather spartan surroundings have probably helped us out a little over the years. It's not a very comfortable place to come to, so it would stand to reason that there might have been a few lads in the opposition dressing room who just didn't fancy it.

*

I've been a free-taker for my entire life, which has as much to do with the fact that I was often the only left-footed forward in the team as it does with any particular aptitude for that task on my part. Being a free-taker can give you a very specific perspective on your home ground. If you're a free-taker, then you will spend more time by yourself down at the pitch than any other member of your team. The more you practise, the more of an understanding you cultivate of every blade of grass inside both forty-five-yard lines. There's a prevailing wind that you have to get used to. A dip in the surface at a certain spot, a look at the goalposts from a certain angle that just never sits right with you.

The pitch can be a refuge – a place to walk to with a bag of balls to just forget about everything else in your life, where you don't have to engage with anyone. Just yourself, six O'Neill's footballs and an opportunity to quietly visualize whatever game it is that you're preparing for. I've always loved that. As much as a solitary kicking session like that is about simply free-taking, it's also often the first act in the weekend's football for me: once I have that session done, I can say that I'm ready for the following day's action. If I miss my first free, I won't be kicking myself for a lack of preparation. I don't know what players who aren't responsible for taking frees do to get themselves in that frame of mind, but in those situations the pitch is quite literally the only place I want to be. Spending too long down there is the only danger.

The more I practise on a pitch, the more I become convinced that it – that every pitch – has a 'scoring' goal: an end where, owing to the microclimate created by whatever combination of wind and light and visual backdrop and pitch conditions, it's easier to put the ball between the posts. I am far from alone in this belief; it is widely held in the GAA. Jim Carney's match reports from Tuam Stadium made regular reference to the scoring goal there: the one closest to the town (or the one on the right-hand side of the screen, if you're watching on TG4). Jim reckoned it had to be worth three or four points in every game.

The nature of the microclimate that produces a 'scoring' goal may be more psychological than physical. One end of the pitch will be a little closer to the dressing room used by the home team than the other. Or one goal will have nets behind it, thereby making it a lot easier for the chronically lazy free-taker in the group to retrieve their own attempts. They'll often be the first player out for training, so their teammates will join them at that end. Soon everyone feels more comfortable hitting into that goal. They will decide that there's some magical advantage to be gained by shooting into that goal. The opposition will note that the home team prefer to shoot into that goal, and that information will also seep into their consciousness. Before you know it, you have a scoring goal on your hands.

When driving past GAA clubs, I can never help looking in over the wall: is it a good set-up, is it a grand set-up, is it an *unbelievable* set-up? The fact that there are thousands of other rubberneckers doing likewise as they drive through Milltown is at least part of the reason it's so well kept now.

People often say that a GAA club is the glue holding a community together – but what does that mean exactly? It is something created in a community, for the benefit of that community, out of which no one gets any material enrichment or even, in many cases, any personal glory. A GAA club downplays individual achievement and emphasizes the success of the collective. Not only is it set up for the community, it also assumes the name of the community. The idea of Milltown the village is interchangeable with Milltown the GAA club. No one calls it Milltown GFC. Milltown is the club, and Milltown is the village.

Sociologists use the concept of the 'third place'. In Ray Oldenburg's 1989 book *The Great Good Place*, the third place is defined as 'a generic designation for a great variety of public places that host the regular, voluntary, informal, and happily anticipated gatherings of individuals beyond the realms of home and work'. In this formulation then, the first place is home, the second place is work. For many people in Ireland, the third place is the GAA club.

Home and work, Oldenburg writes, serve to 'cloister people among their own kind', but a third place is about providing a space where people of different generations, different social classes, and different belief structures can meet and do things together. It's not important that everyone in a third place agrees with each other on everything, it's simply important that they understand the importance of community and common purpose.

When I go to weddings or social events in my peer group, I often find myself praying that I'm sitting beside my close friends, and not left 'isolated' with people I know less well. When I worked in an office with fifty other people in Newstalk, I found myself breaking out in a cold sweat at the thought that I'd be left alone at social gatherings with anyone other than the five or six people I worked closely alongside in the sports department.

By contrast, when I walk into the dressing room before a football game, I don't care who I sit beside. When we go to the pub as a team to celebrate a victory, I purposely seek out people on our team I haven't spoken that much to in the previous few weeks to drink with.

My friend Collie McKeown frequently teases me for being scared stiff of walking into a pub by myself without knowing that someone from the group of friends I'm going to meet is in there before me. I would send multiple text messages to ensure someone had arrived before I got there, so I wouldn't be forced to stand at the bar drinking by myself.

And yet I walk down to the pitch in Dolphin's Barn if the thirds are playing or the men's or women's seniors are playing, and I don't need to know there's one of my close friends down there before I set off. I walk down, and I know I'll fall into conversation with someone on the sideline. If it's someone I don't know, I'll be introduced or I'll introduce myself, and I'll happily stand there and chat to anyone who passes by.

At work, I suppose that might be termed networking, or relationship-building. Either way, it's something that you're doing while getting paid for it. I don't know if it is simply the removal of the financial element that makes this sort of interaction at a GAA match different from a chat at the office microwave, but it is different. There is a definite sense that what happens in that situation on the sideline is a strengthening of the nexus that makes the club – not my one-to-one relationship with that person, but another strand linking the team I play with to the club executive, or the women's second team, or to the under-15 team that someone's son or daughter plays on.

On a beautifully sunny evening in the summer of 2022, I went down to watch our thirds play a league match. After the game I stayed behind, talking to a couple of my friends on the team. I was introduced to Löic, a Frenchman who had moved to Dublin a couple of years ago. He had sought out the club on social media, and joined to play and train with our fourth team. Directly behind us was another man involved in the club who I hadn't yet been introduced to. It was Tom Ryan, the director general of the GAA: the most powerful role in the entire association. A church doesn't get much broader than that.

11. Bringing Someone In

To the outside world, there appears to be no bolder statement that a club is about to start taking things seriously than the news that they are 'bringing someone in'. There's going to be a new sheriff in town. They've gone and found an outside manager.

The outside manager is presented as the panacea. What these lads need, the thinking goes, is someone who'll tell it to them straight. No more favourites, no more indulgences, no more bullshit. Everyone should be shifting uncomfortably in their seats . . . even the players – and there were probably four or five of them – who went and met this fella before he was hired.

Of course, we'll have to put a few of our own people with him as selectors, a couple of lads to lay out the cones before training, and maybe one or two truth-tellers to let him know that obviously we're all for a new broom around the place, that's why we brought you in . . . but Jesus, you can't drop that lad, he was a county minor eight years ago.

In truth, the hiring of an outside manager is not always a bold statement of intent. Sometimes it's a last resort, when no plausible candidate within the club is willing to take the job. In this scenario, more often than not, it will be the players who will be left with the task of asking around and trying to find a victim. Lads working in a neighbouring county will keep their ear to the ground to see if there's someone who had taken over a club in the doldrums and ripped it up in that county's championship the season before.

Inquiries will be made. Uncomfortable conversations around money will be had. Accommodations will be reached. A man will be hired, and inside two or three weeks the players will know whether the new manager is a spoofer or not. Sometimes it doesn't even take that long. Because for every talented, dedicated coach eager to make his way in that game, there is a man of dubious talent, or dubious work-ethic, or both, who will take your club's money and run.

Things can get tricky when – at club or county level – an outside appointment is seen to be blocking the development of a young in-house coach. That's when someone will ask the question: If players are bound by the 'parish rule', why should it be any different for managers?

The metric was very simple for Brian Cody. You manage your own club, you manage your own county, and doing anything else is a perversion of what makes the GAA great. The country tied itself up in knots in 2022 when Cody had a long, lingering, wordless handshake with Henry Shefflin – the greatest of many great players in Cody's Kilkenny dynasty, his on-field lieutenant, his own relentless winning mentality made flesh inside the white lines – after Shefflin's Galway beat Kilkenny by a point in the Leinster Hurling Championship in Pearse Stadium. And after Kilkenny won the Leinster final between the two teams later that summer, Cody wandered around Croke Park avoiding having to shake Shefflin's hand, until Shefflin ended the charade by marching over to him and offering his congratulations.

Denis Walsh, then of the *Sunday Times*, watching the handshake in Salthill, immediately recalled something Cody had said to him during his first season in charge of Kilkenny.

Talking about his selector Ger Henderson, Cody said: 'He was dedicated to his club at home, which appeals to me. He's loyal – a Johnstown man and a Kilkenny man. I'm a Village man, a James Stephens man, and I think that's the way it should be. Lots of people go around training other teams and I can't see how they can do that too easily.'

It is a very simple outlook, and a very easy position to take if you happen to be the Kilkenny manager while you're saying it. But waiting around for Brian Cody to be finished as Kilkenny manager can't have seemed a very attractive option to Henry Shefflin, or to Eddie Brennan, or Michael Fennelly, or any of the rest of the players that played under him for years and were anxious to advance their coaching careers. Cody was in the job for almost a quarter of a century, and it was still a shock when he left. And having to face Henry Shefflin on the sideline managing a team *against* Kilkenny, twice in his last summer, was a betrayal . . . as far as Cody's moral compass was concerned.

If what Cody did for Kilkenny hurling is unrivalled, it should also be acknowledged that he elevated the game nationally also. He prepared teams to play hurling at a standard that we'd never seen before. The fact that his world-view would preclude his own players from trying to inculcate those standards in counties other than Kilkenny could be seen as a massive opportunity lost for the sport as a whole. Galway hurling (and Laois hurling, and Offaly hurling, and Kildare hurling) has learned plenty from having ex-Cody hurlers in charge over the past five years.

Outside managers have been widely used at club and county level for decades. In the 2023 Leinster Hurling Championship, five of the six managers were from outside the county they were managing. It's obvious that the best man or woman for the job is not always to be found inside the county lines. The few who have the dedication and the skill set to do it well view coaching as a vocation – not merely as an act of local service. And yet a coach's vocation is often sneered at in the GAA. There is a widespread view that what really drives these people is the desire for a few quid.

The practice of paying a coach or manager a cash amount per training session has always been against the rules, but it has nevertheless been going on unimpeded for decades. The average 'outside' club coach, to the best of my knowledge, gets somewhere in the region of €150 per session. There are plenty of people taking in that sort of money. I have no idea what a county manager can charge a county board – one hears much speculation on the subject, as well as some outright lies – but it must be at least twice that per session. If the manager takes three training sessions a week (a conservative estimate) from mid-November to mid-June (another conservative estimate), that adds up to €27,900.

Keep in mind your manager might be a different person from your coach. An inter-county coach might be getting a flat rate of €300 a session as well: that's another €27,900. If we add the mileage costs the county board must pay – which can get into the five figures per annum if the manager lives a significant distance from the training ground – it's an extraordinary outlay for a county board to take on, let alone one they feel duty-bound to hide from public view.

The bare fact of the matter is that if you're in charge of a team, at club or county level, and it's not the team you grew up playing for or the club you're currently affiliated to, people presume you're getting paid. This runs contrary to the proclaimed ethos (and the rule book) of the GAA. But it's there in plain sight. I have been at managerial unveilings where a prominent local businessman, whose name is nowhere near the county jersey as main sponsor, is thanked for his help in getting the high-profile name into the county. What sort of help are we talking about here, exactly? Do we need to be drawn a diagram? And shouldn't there at least be a degree of shame involved?

The feeling persists that taking money from your own county is not quite cricket – which is not to say it's never done. Rightly or wrongly, I happen to believe that plenty of the best-known managers in the game don't take anything other than the expenses that are rightly owing to them, purely because they are managing their own county.

If a club or a county pays its manager, then it's breaking the rules of the association. (And if they're not declaring it to the Revenue, they're breaking the laws of the land.) And, if a club *is* paying its manager, who will investigate and prosecute this flagrant abuse of the most cherished value of the entire GAA, amateurism? The county board. But if that county board is breaking the rules also, by paying (or having in the past paid) its own manager, then it might not carry out too thorough an investigation.

If clubs are acutely aware of their own county boards' hypocrisy in relation to payments to managers, then those same clubs are likely to look at how a county board attempts to enforce the rules of the association in other ways, perhaps in relation to violent conduct. If the law is 'do as I say, not do as I do', then it never takes long for a county board to collapse under the weight of its own hypocrisy.

Perhaps the answer is to lift the ban on paying managers. It is not self-evident that this would strike a fatal blow against the GAA's amateur ethos. Many of the people on the sideline at big games in Croke Park – physiotherapists, doctors, sports psychologists, etc. – are paid already.

My old NUI Galway history professor Gearóid Ó Tuathaigh has been a prominent commentator on this for years. When I asked him about it, he made a distinction between people being given recompense for *expertise* (such as those physios, doctors, sports psychologists I've just referenced) and those being given recompense for *time*. The point is not that managers and coaches lack expertise. The point is that their expertise – unlike that of doctors and physios – is not of any financial value outside the GAA. The expertise of a physiotherapist is a service that we pay for in regular society. If a player got injured at a training session with no physiotherapist present, they would have to go to a physio clinic and pay for treatment (or pay and be reimbursed by their county board). The expertise of a GAA manager is relevant only within the bounds of the GAA, an amateur organization. I think it's a valuable, instructive distinction.

But what then to make of county board officials? Most counties now have at least one full-time officer, to supplement the efforts of volunteer members of the county executive. These officers receive salaries. Why is their full-time work, and their compensation, not deemed to be a breach of the GAA's amateur ethos?

This is a rather more difficult needle to thread. The practice of paying salaries to county board officials dates back thirty years or more, and it was given the official stamp of approval by the 2002 Strategic Review Committee, which made it GAA organizational policy to hire full-time staff to help run county boards. The explanation given to me in conversations with veteran administrators is that there was a dawning realization that the job was becoming too much for men and women who also had to try and hold down a day job. More and more was being asked of volunteers – issues relating to handling government funding, disbursing grants from Sport Ireland, Garda vetting of coaches, and the negotiating of seven-figure commercial deals, among other things. In short, the job became too much for a person to do in their spare time. When that became clear, the GAA allowed those people to be paid.

It's hard to argue that we're not on the same road with the role of the inter-county manager. Even high-profile counties can have difficulty in finding candidates to take on management roles, given the arduous workload involved. Perhaps a properly regulated system of payment would sweeten the deal somewhat. It would at least satisfy the Revenue – and I find it hard to believe that earning forty or fifty grand a year in undeclared payments isn't a worry for at least some prospective managers and coaches. Those people making the choice to get involved in inter-county teams could then make a judgement on the merits of a binding contract, signed and respected by both parties, that would regulate and normalize what is presently a free-for-all. But maybe we have stumbled upon the most compelling reason for the GAA's inability to deal with this issue: there are currently too many people earning too much money tax-free for anyone to tackle it for good.

There is the possibility of a tax exemption being negotiated on behalf of GAA managers. Rugby players get them, if they stay and play their rugby in the country, and artists get them, so why not GAA managers? The result would be less chicanery for the GAA, more certainty and less ducking and diving for managers, and a bit of a tax take for the Revenue from the best-paid managers – not the worst deal, all told.

Some inter-county managers are probably very happy to be paid tax-free. Others might feel uncomfortable about being on the wrong side of the Revenue – and having to stay there because to declare their income would mean implicating their county boards in tax evasion. It's not just the recipient of these funds that is on the wrong side of tax law, or any concept of good governance. The money being paid surreptitiously to managers should exist somewhere on a balance sheet, and it doesn't. County boards have to find ways to hide it on the books, or ensure managers are paid by non-affiliated supporters' groups or sponsors. How can we say we're interested in hiring only the best and brightest to run our county boards if they won't even be able to say what money was spent on whom at the end of any given year? And there can hardly be effective oversight when no county board meeting will be presented with the final cost of hiring a manager, no budget can be drawn up and realistically referred back to throughout the season, and no record can ever exist of a contract drawn up between the two parties.

There might be a subset of players who believe that they, too, deserve to be paid. But the drive for players to be paid has lost all momentum in recent years. At the moment, inter-county players are reasonably well looked after with mileage rates, a government grant that 'recognizes their contribution to the Irish economy', and, for the top rank, as much sponsorship as corporate Ireland deems their profile to be worth. Perhaps there's a recognition there that the crowds and the sponsorship and the TV rights don't bring in enough money to pay every inter-county player, male and female, the sort of money that would allow them to become full-time.

Amateurism has its benefits for GAA players. Their ability to progress their off-field career at the same time as their sporting career, and the widespread availability of college GAA scholarships under the system currently in place, means that the average male GAA inter-county player aged thirty-two or thirty-three is in a much better position than a League of Ireland footballer of a similar age. There are, of course, challenges to their work–life balance, but GAA players at least have a route onto the rungs of the ladder they see themselves climbing, while they pursue their sporting careers. How far they climb up that ladder is a different matter, but they're at least not being thrown out of the workforce in their mid-thirties with no idea of what the next step is.

Would the open payment of managers at inter-county level damage the 'associational culture of volunteerism', as Professor Ó Tuathaigh put it to me? My instinctive answer is no. The volunteers who run clubs have taken the professionalization of Croke Park operations in their stride. They have seen paid chief executives at county board level and accepted that. I think there's a growing realization among those same volunteers that inter-county managers are putting in the sort of hours that make it almost impossible for them to hold down a regular job. I would not anticipate widespread manning of the barricades if the decision was made to regulate inter-county managerial payments.

But taking their efforts for granted would be a major misstep. No one believes for a second that the GAA would survive a day without volunteers. Paying people to manage club teams might not be the straw that breaks this particular camel's back, but it would be dangerous to assume that the camel could take a whole lot more than that. A fear of endangering that spirit of volunteerism is the reason why nobody in the GAA argues that clubs ought to be able to pay their managers.

Ten years ago, GAA director general Páraic Duffy produced a discussion document on the potential payment of county managers. It was a darkly comic episode in the life of the GAA. He wrote of the workload involved: 'It is conceivable that many team managers devote, in terms of hours, the equivalent of a full working-week to their function during the playing season (which covers the period of preparation that precedes the playing season), and this, often, on top of their own full-time employment commitments.' The workload of inter-county managers has only increased since then.

He acknowledged that the GAA had a problem with under-the-table payments to managers. He asked the membership a very direct question. Should we (a) attempt to come up with a system whereby managers can be paid a fair, agreed wage for their services; (b) crack down on illegal payments and reassert our adherence to the idea of amateurism; or (c) do nothing, stick our heads in the sand and pretend nothing's wrong? The following year he came back to Congress and made sure to remind everyone there that the resounding answer he'd gotten to this question was (c). It epitomized the sort of bracingly straightforward attitude that Duffy brought to the role. He can at least say he tried to grasp the nettle.

12. Being There

'I've two tickets to the game on Sunday, will you go?' The text arrives on a Thursday. I tell myself that this will be an occasion to remember: the 2021 Connacht semi-final in Dr Hyde Park during a global pandemic. Yes, I will go.

Sunday starts in glorious sunshine in Dublin 8. I mean, sure, the weather app says there's a 90 per cent chance of rain in Roscommon later on, but it's sunny right now, where I am – it just doesn't compute with me that, in just three short hours, I could be sitting in a biblical deluge in Roscommon. And anyway, that iPhone weather app is a laughing stock. I throw my (light, summery, entirely ineffectual-in-a-freak-weather-event) jacket in the back seat, but I pack the sun-cream as well, just in case.

While I'm on the road, my brother picks up the tickets from the Athenry chairman. Hmmm . . . the ticket says it's uncovered seating. It sounds like we'll be on the terrace on the opposite side of the pitch, facing the main stand, but that's OK. There's a roof along the back of that terrace, we'll be grand if (if!) a bit of rain lands in for a few minutes.

I arrive in Roscommon, and the rain has come a couple of hours early. It feels like we're in a car-wash. It clears a little about twenty minutes before throw-in, and we breathe a sigh of relief . . . thank Christ we didn't get caught in that.

I check the boot for the umbrella I've kept in there for the last two years. It's not there. In fact, that umbrella might never have been in my boot. That could just have been a trick of the mind. I feel like I'm the sort of outdoorsman who would always have an umbrella in the boot. But this is a minor setback. The deluge is already over, we've dodged a bullet.

We walk into the ground, and it turns out uncovered really means uncovered. We're sitting on the wide open terraced seating in front of the main stand. That's OK though, the sun's out. Bloody hell, I left my sunglasses in the car . . . silly, silly man. I'm squinting furiously here.

Two minutes before the game starts, the rains come. After fifteen minutes I am wet through. That's OK: 'Once you're wet, you're wet', as my dad used to say. There aren't degrees of wetness. Your jeans are wet, your jacket is wet, what more can water do to you, realistically? As the ball is thrown in for the second half, someone somewhere turns the rain up a notch. To quote the writer Kevin Barry, it was by now a hysterical downpour.

I realize that my father (happily ensconced in the stand behind me, bone dry) was wrong: you can always get wetter. That first moment when you realize that water is now running playfully between your butt-cheeks is a sobering one. Rain starts to gather in my crotch, in my armpits . . . my armpits! I didn't know that was possible.

We stare intently from our uncovered seats in front of the stand across to the entirely empty terrace on the opposite side, the terrace with a (small, but no doubt extremely effective) roof running along the back. I devote seconds, minutes to staring at that corrugated iron roof. I calculate how many people could be huddled underneath that roof while maintaining social distancing. I luxuriate in the maths, I bathe myself in the numbers.

The game happens in front of me, but it is hard to focus on anything other than the constant threat of pneumonia.

Someone mentions extra time. Dark thoughts cloud my mind. I think of poor Michael Furey, in 'The Dead' by James Joyce, who caught his death outside Gretta Conroy's window. That'll be me now, dying of consumption over a football game. Wait, wasn't Michael Furey from Oughterard? Galway's second goal-scorer, Matthew Tierney, is from Oughterard – and in many ways his last act in this . . . oh Jesus Christ! I'm going delirious.

The game finishes. Galway have won, at least. This comforts me, even as it becomes clear from the incessant beeping of my phone that I have been caught on television celebrating the aforementioned Tierney goal wearing a look of bewilderment and simplicity that accurately sums up my extremely scattered mental state.

I trudge back to the car, and anxiously scan my boot to see if there are any scraps of clothes I can put on me. Surely there's some football gear, another rain jacket, a pair of socks even. My eyes alight on my wife's Dryrobe. I take off my jacket. Then I take off my T-shirt. I pop on the Dryrobe. The legends are true – this truly is a miracle of science. I can dry myself with it, as I'm wearing it? What could anyone possibly have against such a garment?

I sit into the driver's seat. Hmmm . . . my jeans are still pretty wet. This Dryrobe goes well past my waist. Maybe I could just . . . yes, the jeans will come off. Must come off, in fact. I drive home entirely naked save for a Dryrobe, and my shoes and socks. I am reminded, as my car's air conditioning blasts heat unfettered by cloth or stitch directly to my undercarriage, that nothing beats being there.

A few weeks after the above account of my Roscommon misadventures appeared in the *Irish Times*, I got a withering text message from a friend of mine, saying that 'supporting your county team is for auld fellas and schoolkids'. The man who told me this watches more GAA than is strictly good for one's health, and has played or been involved at every level of the association, be that club, county, or college, so I didn't immediately dismiss this superior-sounding generalization. (Then again, he's from Cork, where sounding superior is practically an art form.)

So, who actually does support their county team, other than auld fellas and schoolkids? Well auld ladies, for a start. But there is also a cohort expressly left out of that equation: the playing-age population of the GAA, the people in their twenties and thirties who should know and appreciate the hard work required to play at the top level, should have a deeper understanding of the game as it's being played now, and should in fact personally know the players who make up the county team better than almost anyone else.

It seems wrong-headed, but many club players just have no interest in going to inter-county games. This is, at least in part, a symptom of how bad the fixtures situation was for twenty years or so until the recent reforms. The only certainty players could provide loved ones was that if their county team is playing on a given weekend, that is one weekend the club team most certainly would not be playing. Essentially, to a percentage of the playing population, the county team was something that stood in the way of them getting to play.

The split season has changed that equation. But there is still a cohort of club players who want their county team beaten so they can get a start made on their own club championship. The longer the county team stays in contention, the louder the calls will be to delay the start of the club championship. These demands should never be listened to but, of course, they often are. 'We can't expect them to just turn around and throw themselves into their club campaigns,' people will often say of county players – but club players will never be asked before being told they will have to change their diaries.

For everyone else, perhaps the county team should be taken as part of a balanced GAA diet – mixing the high-carb experience of Thurles or Croke Park with the fibre-rich goodness of an intermediate club hurling game, as well as the sugar rush of high-quality under-16 stuff (and that's not to mention the thin gruel of under-8 training in the rain in October).

There will always be people who will support their county team through thick and thin. But they're not exactly held up as the purest of the pure – the exemplar for all other sup-porters to follow. More often than not, I find myself good-naturedly running these people down for attending FBD League games in January (or shamefacedly admitting my own lunacy for being there alongside them). For the great majority of GAA people, when your county team is terrible, you can stay away guilt-free and focus on the club. When they're good, you put the bunting up, happily jump in the car, and you're welcomed with open arms. We understand that; in fact, that's how you separate the good years from the lean ones.

All-Ireland final tickets are distributed through the clubs, who reward the people who take teams, who sit on commit-tees, who run the show at home. That annoys those people for whom involvement in the GAA is solely based around supporting their county team, but that's the system. The only way around that is to buy a GAA season ticket, and that, to be honest, is a commitment most of us are happy to avoid.

So, tradition dictates that the county team should be the cherry on top of your engagement with the GAA, not the meat and two veg. You love the journey, you appreciate every day of it, but you can be refreshingly realistic about it. For most of us, our day-to-day GAA existence is taken up with the club. The emotional highs and lows, irrational fears, and unrealistic ambitions are reserved for your local team.

Seeing the GAA purely through the prism of an inter-county team only gives you a narrow view of what it all means. I say that in full knowledge of how lucky I am to have been born in the county I was born in. Each summer, I get to watch our county hurling, camogie, men's and women's football teams, at minor, under-20 and senior level, on television or in the flesh, competing at the very highest level.

In the summer of 2022, Galway teams across all codes were shown playing championship games on RTE, Sky or on TG4 twenty-eight times. One weekend I was able to watch the Galway minor footballers play a Connacht Championship game on TG4's YouTube channel at 7 p.m. on a Friday evening, watch the Galway minor hurlers on Saturday at midday, again on YouTube, and see the Galway senior footballers beat Roscommon on RTE 2 the following day.

It's very different for most other counties. Longford, for example, did not have a single game broadcast on any channel in any code for the entire calendar year. If inter-county fandom was what really counted for GAA people, then the weaker counties would have given up long ago. I'm very grateful the inter-county game can provide the joy it's given me, but I'm also glad it's not the only show in town.

The trials and tribulations (and brilliant football) of the Mayo county team over the past fifteen years or so have captured the attention of even the most casual sports fan. Their support is extraordinary, but it's also a wider church than most other counties. I heard a story from Mike Finnerty, the sports editor of the *Mayo News*, about the days immediately after the 2021 All-Ireland final. Mike presents a Mayo GAA podcast that has become a cult hit. One man who had appeared a few times on the show over the years was an American by the name of Jim Zoldy. Jim had been driving around Mayo on his holidays in 2016, and he passed house after house after house with the green and red flags out. Curious, he asked what the flags signified. He got the full story – all sixty years of it – and that was all he needed. He watched the 2016 final in a pub, was in Croke Park for the 2017 final, and in subsequent years paid uncomfortably large amounts on the black market for tickets. In 2021 he had no luck, due to the Covid-reduced capacity, so he watched the final in a pub in Drumcondra.

He'd booked a couple of days in Mayo to take in any celebrations. Of course, there were to be no celebrations. But he headed west the following day nevertheless. He was walking down the street in Westport a few days after the All-Ireland final when he met Mike Finnerty on the street. Mike had put two of the hardest days of work of his life into that week's edition of the *Mayo News*, and had just walked out of the Fairgreen pub in Westport after a pint to mark the safe passage of the paper to the printers.

Mike talked to Jim for a second, and then told him to wait outside, because, unbeknownst to Jim, the entire Mayo squad were in the pub Mike had just walked out of. Mike went back in, caught Lee Keegan's eye, and asked him will he come out onto the street for five minutes to talk to the man who flew halfway around the world to watch the All-Ireland final in some dingy pub in Dublin 3 . . . and Mayo's greatest ever player was more than happy to oblige.

Suffice to say, that is not the usual GAA fan experience. But then, perhaps there is no standard experience. At the National League final between Mayo and Kerry in 2022, I was behind a woman who was attending the match on her own, even though she was Dublin born and reared, because her husband was from Mayo, and her kids (also Dublin born and reared) had grown up as Mayo fans. They couldn't make it, but this Dublin woman ended up going by herself anyway.

The sheer number of expats living in Dublin makes who your child supports a rather vexed issue. One of my teammates in Templeogue Synge Street is a Mayo supporter, even though he's lived in Dublin for his entire life, because his father is a Mayo fanatic.

That particular route is not entirely one-way: there have been stories of clubs in Meath organizing buses to Croke Park for Dublin supporters as a way of making a few quid. The Dublin supporters are priced out of Dublin, and the culchies in the city are trying to convince their children to support a county other than the county they were born and raised in.

My own support of the Galway senior hurling and football teams is intrinsically linked with my location in Dublin. In years where the hurlers and footballers are both going well, and make it to Croker, that usually means I see my family about three times more often than in summers where they're both out early on.

Galway's exit from the 2019 Leinster Hurling Championship in the last minute to Dublin, because of a draw between Wexford and Kilkenny a hundred kilometres from Parnell

Park, was a definite low point. The previous two summers had been full of Sunday afternoons spent in Croke Park with my nephews and my parents, and this seemed just too cruel and unusual a punishment.

About six months after that traumatic event in Donnycarney, my friend who attended the Galway–Dublin match with me (it might have been his first ever hurling match) was asked apropos of nothing if he'd ever seen me angry. He said the only time he'd ever really seen me lose my cool was in the immediate aftermath of that game, as I was sitting in the passenger seat of his left-hand-drive car (his partner is French) driving down the old Malahide Road. I was busily texting my brothers in disgust at how the day had panned out, and a pedestrian was slow in crossing the road in front of us. He saw me on the right-hand-side of the car, texting away, and instead of scurrying across the road, he gestured at me to put my phone away, presuming that I was texting and driving simultaneously. Before I knew it I was rolling down the window, passive-aggressively shouting, 'It's a left-hand-drive, MATE,' at a bewildered pedestrian. It was at that juncture that my friend correctly surmised that I was not to be engaged with in any way until I had calmed down.

I am, as previously stated, not exactly pure unfiltered 100 per cent proof Galwegian myself. My dad's Waterford heritage obviously means we've a major soft spot for them. But when the time came in the 2017 All-Ireland hurling final, there weren't any mixed feelings. I was desperate for Galway to win, to beat Waterford, regardless of the fifty-eight-year wait since Waterford's last title.

Dad was, of course, supporting Waterford – which may or may not shock you, but which certainly wasn't shocking to us. He has two brothers and a sister still living in the county, and he had gone down to games in the Munster Hurling Championship throughout the 1980s, well after he'd moved to Milltown, to support them in provincial finals in which they'd received truly historically bad beatings (5-31 to 3-6 in 1982, 3-22 to 0-12 in 1983 – both to Cork, games which still induce a shudder whenever they get mentioned).

There was never even a question of his allegiances changing, despite the fact that he has had plenty of good days supporting the Galway hurlers. He has more of a connection with the Galway footballers, given he's trained plenty of young men who wore the jersey over the years, but even at that – if the Waterford footballers ever got their act together, I wouldn't expect him to shout against his own in the big-ball game either.

When I met Dad after that 2017 hurling final, I felt bad for him, but it wasn't a case of divided loyalties. I see it as a major advantage being able to support more than one team in the hurling championship every year, but there is a clear hierarchy. If you have a deep and meaningful relationship with your home place, or even a deep and troubled one, the GAA offers a nice way to try and work that out. But that's not your children's experience of that county.

When Colm Boyle retired after one of the great Mayo football careers, I talked to a few people around Milltown about the rivalry between Boyle's club Davitts and our own, two clubs separated by about four miles . . . and the Galway–Mayo county line.

Boyle grew up in Ballindine, which, along with Irishtown, is the home of Davitts GAA Club, named after Michael Davitt, the founder of the Land League. And if Davitt was not a man to back down from a fight, then the club that bears his name does his memory no disservice.

I remember playing one or two challenge games at under-12 level against them, or maybe younger, but playing them in adult football seemed to be off-limits. There was perhaps something about the onset of puberty that necessitated we be kept apart. I tried to find out from the village elders if there was one incident in particular that led to our tribes being separated like this, but a veil of silence fell and I hastily dropped the matter.

It might have had something to do with a certain long-standing tradition in the vicinity on the evening of Galway–Mayo games. If Galway won, we in Milltown would send our most diplomatically sensitive emissaries to Ballindine and Irishtown, in a spirit of friendship and comity of course, to discuss the game with the locals. If Mayo won, the favour would be zestily returned in the opposite direction. Keeping the lines of communication open was deemed very important, at least on Connacht final night.

Milltown is, ecclesiastically, a half-parish with Ballyglass – part of which is in County Mayo. Much confusion arises from this. The church of Ballyglass is still in Galway, but many of its parishioners live in Mayo, and they would play with Davitts GAA club, in Mayo. Whatever about religion, when you consider the elevated status of football in both communities, it's only natural that the GAA is particularly adept at highlighting the fault lines.

The Davitts catchment area lies flush up against the Galway border. Milltown lies four miles inside the county. So if your nearest school was in Ballindine or Irishtown, then it stood to reason that you would attend that school, and, in time, perhaps play football for the local club with your schoolfellows . . . even if your house was actually in Galway. So there are isolated tales of All-Ireland winning underage

Mayo footballers (not Colm Boyle, I hasten to add) who were actually born and lived in the county of Galway. That may not make sense geographically, but I think this is at least intellectually consistent.

More baffling to me is the Gael, born and living on the Galway side of the border, who is a rabid supporter of Davitts – a club, lest we forget, affiliated to the Mayo county board – but who then also shouts for Galway, against Mayo. One such individual was so vocal in his celebrations of Galway's 1998 All-Ireland win that his jawing precipitated a mass walkout from a pub in Irishtown that night. The local publican, it is said, had to retire to his bed, heartsick at this affront to his sensibilities. The man in question, who was so raucously rejoicing in Galway's win, had been a manager of the Davitts senior team, and his son had even worn the Green and Red with distinction.

Some will say that this attitude, while devastating to one's local pub landlord, is more in keeping with GAA orthodoxy – that this is just another example of the primacy of the club. But I feel like once you've taken geography and convenience into account in choosing the club that is nearest to you – regardless of what parish your house is actually in – then you forfeit the right to swap back those allegiances when it comes to the inter-county game. And, let's face it, Galway might have the edge in All-Ireland titles won, but it's not a choice between a minnow and a titan of the modern game – Galway and Mayo will almost always be at the sharp end of things in the inter-county game. Either way, the mind truly boggles.

And lest you think that such petty border squabbles are of no concern to you, this controversy goes all the way to the top. Sabina Higgins, wife of our current president, has similarly divided loyalties. I quote here directly from President Higgins's official website: 'Sabina Coyne, now Higgins, was born . . . on the Galway–Mayo border and went to school in Ballindine and Claremorris, Co. Mayo.'

Any reasonable person would be inclined to infer from this that she is a Mayo woman. But we in Milltown know different. Mrs Higgins, you can no longer run from this. Even now, for the good of the country, admit the error of your ways, return to the fold.

Galway's run to the All-Ireland football final of 2022 began for me in Sabina's neck of the woods. I got the train down to Claremorris the day before Galway's Connacht quarter-final against Mayo, to attend the removal and the funeral of my dear cousin-in-law's father, who was a proud Roscommon man from just fifteen miles over the road who had lived his entire married life in Irishtown (but let's just leave the Rossies out of this for the moment).

As we exited the funeral parlour, the crowd assembled outside were humming away conspiratorially about the game. I stood there with my two uncles, my two aunts, my parents, a brother and a scatter of cousins, quietly trading opinions back and forth, to see which of them, if any, would pass muster.

On our way back through Milltown, we spied a game in progress. It turned out the Milltown seniors were playing a league game with St Michael's, a club from Galway city – a game so thrilling, and indeed so violent, and with such a positive outcome on all fronts for Milltown, that I felt honour-bound to go to Sheridan's pub at the top of the hill in the village to decompress. I decompressed about eight pints, in fact, and was blown away by the knowledge and insight of every person I talked to about the game coming up the following day.

Now it may be our location on the border that gives us such a keen interest in what goes on in Mayo, but I was surrounded on all sides by people whose day job is something other than to know all this stuff (unlike me), and yet whose insight and memory for past career highlights and performances made a mockery of my own. These were lads about my age, who I definitely don't remember supporting Galway half as much when we were playing club football together as they clearly do now.

As I tried in vain to remember all the revealing insights into the Galway and Mayo teams I heard that night, I walked down the street to join my father and my uncle for a nightcap in Mullarkey's. My uncle was singing 'The West Clare Railway' as I walked in. I slept the sleep of the just, and then went back across the Mayo line to Irishtown the following morning for the funeral mass.

The sun was shining through the stained-glass side-panels of Irishtown church on a beautiful West of Ireland morning, bathing the wall behind the chief celebrant in a riot of colour as he led the congregation in prayers for a Mayo victory. It seemed to matter little to him that the man who'd died was a Roscommon man (albeit one who'd lived in Mayo for the majority of his life), or, indeed, that there were quite a few Galway people in the congregation. In any case, we took it in the spirit in which it was meant.

We went across the road to Bourke's of Irishtown, the public house cleared so comprehensively of paying customers by the antics of the local Galway supporter back in 1998, for the usual post-funeral offer of a drink and some food. I had a pint, and was picked up by my brother Paul, and on we went to Castlebar. We parked up, an hour and a half early for the match, and met a fellow Milltown man on the street. Fergal Nicholson had driven down from Monaghan, where he lives now, and he was killing time too. He fell into step beside us and started quizzing Paul on his new priorities, given that he now lives in Athenry, firmly in hurling country.

'Would you rather see Galway win a Connacht football final, or an All-Ireland hurling final?' When Paul answered confidently in favour of the hurling, Fergal amended the question slightly – an All-Ireland football semi-final, or a hurling final? This one was tougher. Galway last won an All-Ireland hurling title in 2017, whereas the Galway footballers hadn't even made it to a final since 2001.

We love the Galway hurlers, but we live in a dual county without many dual clubs. Lacking an intimate knowledge of the players and their clubs, it is a more detached sort of fandom. With football, on the other hand, we follow every minor team and every under-20 team, and we have a frame of reference from club football into which we can insert all these names.

Paul is immersed in hurling now, because his son Enda is playing for Athenry, and because he's getting more and more involved in the club. But football is still his first love, and he thought long and hard before replying that an All-Ireland football final with Galway in it needed to happen sooner rather than later.

Paul and Enda walked to their seats high up in MacHale Park, but as I inspected my ticket, alongside my good friend Pádraic Flesk, my heart sank. I have already told you about my misadventures in Roscommon at the Connacht semi-final of 2021, when, besides getting drenched, I was caught by a television camera. More recently, in April 2022, I had once again been caught on camera, at the Division 2 league final in Croke Park between the same two teams, seated as I was in the front row of the Hogan Stand, almost directly behind the Roscommon bench.

Twitter allows for screengrabs of oneself looking idiotic to be passed around at lightning speed, and that duly happened again after the league final. When I walked into MacHale Park on that late April day, I found that my seat was located near the front of the stand, directly behind the Galway bench. I was thus in prime position to be once again spied on national television looking like a buffoon.

Flesk's main priority in life is to infuriate and annoy his dearest friends (nothing on earth gives him greater joy), and he had bought me my ticket for the league final. I couldn't shake the nagging suspicion that I'd been set up. The third member of our party was another Milltown man, the former Galway footballer Darren Mullahy, and within about ninety seconds of the game starting he had identified Galway's double-sweeper system that ended up being the talk of the nation.

Watching Darren coldly dissecting the game while Flesk and I were shouting nonsense in the general direction of the playing area, I couldn't help but think how different it is to be there as a retired county man. You are in the tiny minority of people who genuinely understand the work required to even get to a stage like that. You know how close the roars of support are to the groans of disapproval, and you know how intensely annoying supporters like Flesk and me can be.

This gave me no more than a moment's pause, though, as the game unfolded almost spookily well for Galway . . . right up until the last five minutes, when Mayo launched an unlikely and ultimately unsuccessful comeback. When the final whistle eventually went, we could all see what it meant to John Concannon, a clubmate of Darren's and mine, and to Pádraic Joyce, who is a clubmate of Flesk's.

After the initial euphoria died off, I made my way back to Flesk's car (he lives in Dublin too, so he was my lift home). The incessant beeping of my phone led me to conclude that I had once again been spotted on television, presumably celebrating a Galway point like it was the winning Irish penalty in a World Cup final. Flesk was so delighted by this that it confirmed to me that he had indeed set me up for just such a public humiliation.

Duly burned, I stayed away from the Connacht semi-final against Leitrim. In fact, I missed the Connacht final too, although it wasn't for the lack of effort to get there. I had played a game the evening before, had had a few pints afterwards, and thus was not in peak physical condition as I tried to plan a trip westwards with Flesk.

He too was tired, although his was more of a mental, or even spiritual, fatigue – the previous day having been communion day in the national school he is principal of. A number of Covid cases had necessitated four separate masses, every one of which he had to attend. I felt five hours of religious service was enough suffering for one weekend, without the addition of a five-hour round trip in the car.

Watching Galway play Roscommon on television was a delightful way to spend an early summer afternoon in any case – punching the air after Shane Walsh's beautiful first-half goal, waking the dog from her daytime slumber.

Mam and Dad had stayed away from all the games in Connacht, pleading laziness and old age, and it was hard to blame them. And they were more than happy to stick to that plan of action until they realized the All-Ireland quarter-final against Armagh would be on the same weekend as the All-Ireland Féile hurling tournament was to be held in Dublin. (For the uninitiated, Féile is a national tournament, played at under-15 level. Each county holds a Féile tournament to crown their representatives, and then the county champions go forth to the national tournament, where they are split into four divisions. At the national Féile, each group game lasts only twenty minutes, and the whole thing, including semi-finals and finals, is played off in one day.)

My nephew, the aforementioned Enda, had helped Athenry win the Galway Féile, so would be taking part in the national competition in Dublin that weekend, and Mam and Dad were never going to miss seeing their grandson play. They would, in other words, be in Dublin for All-Ireland quarter-final weekend in any case. So I was tasked with finding three good tickets for Croker the day after Féile.

It was Galway–Armagh first, followed by Mayo–Kerry: the tastiest of double bills. Our seats were beautiful, right in the middle of the Lower Hogan Stand, our backs leaning up against the railing of the Ard Chomhairle section where the trophies are handed out after the All-Ireland final. The TV cameras are often trained in that general direction on All-Ireland final day, but I was reasonably sure we'd be safe enough on this occasion. We were seated beside a group of Mayo men, from Knockmore in the north of the county, who were shouting loudly for Galway, even if the majority of Mayo men and women in Croker that day were rather more circumspect. And given how this was pretty close to a full house – by far the biggest crowd Croke Park had held since the beginning of the Covid pandemic – the sense of occasion was even more evident for everyone there. These were the days we'd promised ourselves more of when we were stuck at home.

I consider myself to be a club truther, the sort of person who is always eager to make the case for the club game. But it can't compete with something like Galway–Armagh. It can't even come close.

Armagh started brightly, and led 4–1 about midway through the first half. From there to the end, Galway were great – and there was a realization for the unexpectedly large Galway crowd in the stadium that a really good team was breaking out before our very eyes. The idea that the team were on the verge of announcing themselves back in the big time was incredibly exciting.

When Kieran Molloy drilled a point over as the clock tip-toed into injury time, we were home. We were six points up, we'd won a brilliant game playing some sparkling football, and we were into an All-Ireland semi-final. And then – pandemonium. An attempt at an Armagh point dropped short, the ball was punched ineffectually off the crossbar by the Galway goalkeeper, and Aidan Nugent palmed home a goal.

Galway went four up again with a point from Damien Comer, and then Armagh got their second goal in injury time, when another mistake in the Galway defence allowed Conor Turbitt in. This stuff happens in slow motion when you're helpless in the stand. I looked at Mam when the second goal went in: *This can't be happening.* But we were still ahead, with the eight minutes of injury time played, when Rian O'Neill landed a free from fully sixty yards out on the angle to force extra time.

The massive Armagh crowd went berserk. Everyone around me from Galway was in shock – and then the fight happened. For forty-five seconds as the teams attempted to leave the field on the Cusack Stand side, all hell broke loose. We were directly across the field from it, and saw basically nothing. But when a fragile peace broke out, the realization hit us: we'd thrown it away. We'd been six points up in injury time, and we still hadn't won the game.

The atmosphere in the ground by this stage was kinetic, and not a little frantic. The Armagh fans had been baying for blood at the final whistle. Over in the Cusack Stand, my *Second Captains* colleague Mark Horgan had arrived with his Argentinian brother-in-law Sebas, and Marianne his Argentinian-born niece, for their first trip to Croke Park. They walked in expecting to see the start of Mayo–Kerry, and instead were brought face-to-face with a forty-man brawl . . . which took a degree of explaining. Beside us, one former clubmate of mine was walking up the gangway and just drew his finger across his throat: *We're dead.* But the brawl seemed to suck the life out of both teams: they played the first half of extra time at a snail's pace. They were both gassed. Then, in the second period of extra time, Galway conceded a third goal, Cillian McDaid fired back with a goal almost immediately, and it ended level after extra time. Penalties.

We actually remained reasonably calm throughout the penalties, maybe because from the very first moments it went beautifully for Galway. Shane Walsh scored our first, then Armagh missed their first, and it was done in a matter of minutes. Pure joy. As the players wheeled off in celebration, whoever was in charge of the PA in Croker blared out 'N17' by the Saw Doctors, and it was a moment of utter communion for every Galway person in the ground. The Saw Doctors are, of course, dismissed by the latté-sippers, whippet owners, and *Irish Times* readers that I am usually (let's face it) in lockstep with, but this was just pure elation.

This was what it was all about. I stood in the concourse of the Hogan Stand afterwards and met three or four lads from home, all of us just shaking our heads at the madness of it all. They were having a pint, but I was happy enough just revelling in the moment. Galway had been involved in the game of the year. They'd lost the game at least once, and yet come out on the right side. It was the ultimate gut-check, and they'd got through. And I was so confident they'd beat Derry in the semi-finals that all of a sudden an All-Ireland final appearance for the footballers, the thing we'd speculated on before the game in Castlebar in April without really believing for a moment it was possible, was seventy minutes away.

The lads from Knockmore seemed genuinely delighted for us, in any case. And as we took our seats for the second game, we were more than happy to cheer each Mayo score too . . . once it became clear that Kerry were going to beat them convincingly. In the interval between the two games, they were telling us about how they won't hear a good word said in their village about Osama bin Laden. My interest suitably piqued, they explained.

The 2001 Mayo county final was set for Sunday, 16 September. Knockmore's best player, and indeed one of the best forwards Mayo have produced in the last fifty years, was Kevin O'Neill, who was at that time (as he still is today) carving out a massively successful career in high finance. He was booked to fly from his part-time home in New York on Wednesday, 12 September to ensure he was fit and rested for the county final.

Then, just before he was due to travel, fate intervened in the form of 9/11. O'Neill spent seventy-two hours in JFK Airport as the twin towers smouldered, finally arrived back in Shannon that Sunday morning, only reached Castlebar at midday, and was unable to work his customary magic. Knockmore drew the game and lost the replay three weeks later, and the blame lies squarely on bin Laden's shoulders.

The story, which was told with a lot of colour, rather put me in mind of a headline that supposedly appeared in the *Tuam Herald* in the 1950s: 'Thousands feared dead in Japan earthquake – local priest uninjured.' All news is local, when it comes down to it.

I left my parents on Clonliffe Road as they strolled back to my aunt's house in Glasnevin and wandered the streets, trying to regulate my breathing. None of the lads from Milltown were hanging around for a pint, so I just kept walking and ended up in Walsh's of Stoneybatter. As I waited for Mark to join me, I sat there with a pint of Guinness and a packet of crisps and tried to put it all in perspective. Seventy minutes from a first All-Ireland football final in twenty-one years.

The following week, the Galway hurlers were playing Limerick in the All-Ireland semi-final, and my brother Paul was up again, with his son Enda. Enda was on the Galway under-15 hurling panel, so hurling is going to be a pretty big deal in both his life and ours for the next five or ten years, it's safe to say. And so while there may not have been too many Galway football fans who came up for the quarter-final, the hurling semi-final, and then the football semi-final in consecutive weeks, Paul was certainly one of them.

Galway were really exceptional, but lost by a couple of points after being level with the all-conquering Limerick going into the last five minutes. All day, Paul was saying hello to lads from Athenry, to lads from other clubs. He's the PRO in the club now, and it struck me that he'll be as heavily involved in the hurling side of things as we have been for the past forty years with football in the county. To put it bluntly, if there were 10,000 Galway football fans at a match, as a family we'd back ourselves to be able to name the club to which at least 1,000 of those were affiliated, maybe more.

When the camera cuts to a crowd scene during a Galway game, I just presume I'm going to know a few faces. Galway is a big county, and yet it's the same faces in Tuam Stadium for club games that are in Pearse Stadium for Galway games. To see Paul gradually morphing into our dad, with his 'How are they all in Kilconieron?' shtick, was quietly hilarious to me.

We had harboured dreams of a double, and the hurlers had given us plenty of reason to hope during that game, but it was all down to the footballers now, and their semi-final against Derry was six days later.

Mam and Dad were up again. Having informally decided to stop attending inter-county games earlier that same summer, they were now out of retirement with a vengeance. With about twenty minutes of ordinary time left in the Armagh game, Dad had leaned over to me and said, 'We'd take two more good tickets for the semi-final if you could get them.' I had been promised three tickets for us all in a corporate box on the Monday after the Armagh game, but as the week progressed, that promise became an expectation, which was subsequently downgraded to a chance . . . and in the end, the tickets never materialized. As the realization dawned late on in that week that I'd need to find a solution for my parents, I called in a favour and got them two tickets in the premium level. Meanwhile, I would be at the match with John, a friend of my brother's from Kinvara – the heart of hurling country.

It was perhaps not a bad day to be separated from Mam and Dad, because as the match unfolded I had little doubt that Derry's style of football would be driving them demented. After twenty-two minutes, Galway trailed 3–0. Galway got back into it by half-time and trailed by a point after a Shane Walsh wide from a forty-five that had been originally given as a point by the umpires was overruled by Hawk-Eye. As I queued to go to the bathroom, all the talk was that the forty-five had in fact gone over, and before long I was peering over a fella's shoulder outside the bathroom, watching video of the incident on Twitter.

By the time I'd gotten back to my seat, John had seen the video evidence too. He looked a little shook. 'They'll surely give us that point – they have to,' I said. 'Never mind this week,' he said, 'what about the two fucking points we were robbed of last week against Limerick?' The hurlers had been at the wrong end of a couple of dodgy-looking Hawk-Eye calls the week before, and . . . well, as Galway hurling or football fans, we all wear the same jersey, but we're all also allowed play favourites. John's heart would always be with the small ball, when push came to shove.

Damien Comer's two second-half goals sealed the Galway win. It seemed almost anticlimactic, given how poor the game had been. But my confidence in Galway beating Derry had been well placed, and we were in the final. We could sit back and enjoy the second semi-final between Dublin and Kerry, which was on the following day.

Getting good tickets for these games is seldom easy. All the clubs in the competing counties are given an allocation from their county boards. There is then a good amount of tickets released for sale online for all games up to the All-Ireland finals. If you're eager just to be inside the gates, regardless of where you are in the stadium, then more often than not you'll find a way. Where it gets complicated is when you have two extremely fussy pensioners, with declining eyesight, who want their seats to be as close to halfway as possible, so they're not straining the entire length of the field to see what's happening at the opposite goal. To be honest,

I'm with my parents on this one. The pitch in Croke Park is 145 metres from end to end, and you can be a long, long way from the action if you don't know where you're buying your ticket for.

The online ticket situation is also fraught. The GAA and Ticketmaster have an infuriating habit of releasing the worst seats first, so you can be rewarded for your eagerness with a seat in the gods, or in the corner of the stand. There were no good tickets for sale online for Galway–Derry, and I wanted my parents to be assured of a good spot. But I knew Mam and Dad were going to stay in Dublin with my aunt Mary on the Saturday night in any case, so I went online on the Friday morning to see if there were any tickets available for the Kerry–Dublin game on Sunday.

If, as I expected, the last remaining seats were of a poor quality, I would buy a couple and see if one of my mates fancied accompanying me. To my shock, I saw that the best seats in the house, pretty much exactly the same ones as we'd sat in for the Galway–Armagh game, were available online. I couldn't quite believe it. I can only speculate as to how these tickets ended up back in circulation. My best guess is that they were corporate tickets that had gone unclaimed. In any case, I didn't hang about questioning how they got there – I bought a pair, and asked Dad if he fancied it. I shouldn't have doubted him.

Dad doesn't go many places without Mam now. His Parkinson's means that, while he's perfectly capable and independent around the house, he struggles with his movement in big crowds, and in places with too many steps. It's only when you're travelling with someone of reduced mobility that you realize just how good-hearted so many people are. Too often I'm on auto-pilot while Mam is quietly guiding

Dad around. In her absence, I grasped the small kindnesses required to ease his passage from place to place. But we were back, the ground was almost entirely full, and it was pure magic.

By the time the pre-match parade started directly in front of us, I had gotten a little emotional. My mind wandered back to 1991, and the All-Ireland final he threw me over the turnstiles for, and how I was blown away by the noise and the colour of the Hill during the parade. And here we were again, thirty-one years later, still in thrall to it all.

The game was a classic, with Sean O'Shea's free from the end of the earth winning it for Kerry in the last minute. After the rather turgid fare of the night before, this had been a raucous, full-blooded, error-strewn but massively dramatic feast of football. I walked Dad back to Glasnevin and my aunt Mary's place again, and was hit by another wave of emotion as I left them. It had been a wonderful day, and we had an All-Ireland final against Kerry to look forward to at the end of it.

We had paid our dues, and then some. We had seen Wexford beat Galway in front of certainly fewer than 1,000 people in Pearse Stadium, in an All-Ireland qualifier at two o'clock on a Saturday afternoon. We had gone to enough terrible league games, enough Mayo hammerings, and enough spirit-crushing defeats to Roscommon to merit whatever level of mania we could muster for this All-Ireland final.

And I certainly was more than a little manic. By Tuesday of All-Ireland final week, I had WhatsApped my potential match-ups to upwards of thirty people. (For months afterwards, I would go to text someone and be reminded that I'd sent them my full tactical breakdown of the Kerry attack in the ten or so days before the All-Ireland final, whether they'd asked for it or not.)

My brother Paul's best friend, John Connolly, who grew up two fields over from us, had returned to Ireland from Boston for the first time in three years. Paul and Connolly have lived in different countries for twenty years now, but Paul never has to wait too long after the final whistle of a Galway game for a message from Boston. Connolly follows it as closely now as he ever did, and as they both got married and had children, on different continents, Galway football was the thing they still talked about more than anything else. And Connolly's younger brother was the head of Galway's statistics team.

John had booked his flight after Galway had beaten Mayo in the Connacht quarter-final in April, which was the sort of hopelessly optimistic act that many fans could appreciate – 'If I'm coming home, I'm just gonna make sure it's not a week too soon, or a week too late, to see something really amazing.' Connolly's arrival home did not calm my nerves – in fact, the sense that the stars were aligning was becoming almost overpowering. I spent most of that week on the phone, inventing ticket dramas and logistical obstacles just to remain in thrice-daily contact with my family.

The evening before the final, my *Second Captains* colleague Eoin McDevitt and I were part of a panel discussion at the Galway Arts Festival. After we'd finished our talk, I walked back into town from NUIG and found myself in the pub explaining to the journalist Róisín Ingle and the archivist and writer Catriona Crowe what an All-Ireland football final appearance means. The crushing weight of one's own tiresomeness is sometimes almost too much to bear.

The Arts Festival gig meant that, for the first time in a very long time, I would be part of the convoy from Galway to Dublin on a big-match morning. I had my wife warned that we were going to be on the road by 8 a.m., and I was awake before my alarm, notwithstanding the few pints we had had the night before. I was aflame with nerves and emotion.

We sat in the car, and we were back in our house in Kilmainham by 10.30. I don't want to overstate how unbearable I had become by this juncture, but it had been a long week. I had told Gill that she was more than welcome to attend, that we'd be able to get her a ticket – and she'd already been at the 2015, 2017 and 2018 All-Ireland hurling finals Galway had played in.

She had loved the 2017 and 2018 finals, but the memory of her off-handedly telling me to 'give it up, this game is over' about ten minutes into the second half of the 2015 final (when the game was, without any doubt, already decided in Kilkenny's favour) was still fresh in both our minds. Would a similar slip of the tongue on this day end our marriage? She decided the best thing to do was to leave the country, and she booked a flight to visit her parents in Yorkshire. The consequences of this decision would only make themselves clear later, but it certainly increased the likelihood that, if this day went the way I hoped it would, I would wake up on Tuesday morning on the floor in Taaffe's bar on Shop Street in Galway city.

I had a shower, got changed, said my goodbyes to Gillian with her best wishes (and an unspoken 'please God let this not go to a replay, I can't stand another two weeks of this') ringing in my ear, and zipped across to Mary's place in Glasnevin again – where so many of these days had started.

I arrived early, but I wasn't the first one there. My cousins Tomás and Niall had arrived, with Niall's girlfriend Meghan and Tom's best friend. Paul was driving Mam and Dad, and he had Connolly and Enda in the car too. They arrived soon after.

My eldest brother, Brian, and his son Adam were next, and then my uncle Jim Carney and his grandson Jamie. All of us were fed. None of us could sit down for long, and in the end we departed in convoy: Mam, Dad, Jim and Jamie in a taxi, to save the ancient legs, and the rest of us on foot. Mary had decided, after almost sixty years of attending Galway All-Ireland finals, that she was going to watch this one at home. It felt wrong to be walking out the door without her, but she wasn't for turning.

Connolly hadn't been in Croke Park since the All-Ireland final of 2001. Paul hadn't been at an All-Ireland football final since then either, which had shocked me when he'd told me earlier in the week. Maybe it's the job that I have, or maybe it's just the fact that I live in Dublin, but I had presumed he'd been back to a final since then. But no – it was his sixth football final, all of them having featured Galway, and he'd been thrown over the turnstiles for his first one too, in 1983.

Most of us were in the Cusack Stand, and so once we were through the gates, we stood just inside the perimeter wall and looked at each other for five or ten minutes. What will we do if we win this thing? We'll meet back here, I suppose? As is often the case before monumental events in your life, it seemed almost unbelievable that time was moving at its normal rate.

There was little else for it but to get to our seats. I was with Mam and Dad again. Galway had no injury concerns, no one to cast your eye over nervously during the warm-up, to see if he was moving OK. Time moved very quickly then, from the warm-up to the presidential salute to the parade. No emotions, no tears, just some nerves, but also a sense of pure joy that we were back at this level. And then the game was on.

It will be remembered as the Clifford–Walsh final of 2022, and with good reason. From the opening minutes it became clear that the two best footballers in the country were intent on putting on a show, and for people who truly love Gaelic football, it was an expression of what the game can be when performed at a higher level than maybe we've ever seen before.

Shane Walsh finished the day with nine points: four from play, four from frees, and a forty-five. Clifford got one point less, but got Sam Maguire. There were spells where it seemed the spotlight was only on those two, and the other twenty-eight players (the best players in the country!) were window-dressing. These were the year's two best teams, and yet it was like an under-16 match between two sides who have each got a forward so good that no one else even gets a look-in.

There's no point in denying it: the beauty of Walsh's performance (and it was genuinely beautiful, I think – like something by Nureyev) made defeat a little easier to swallow. Galway had shown up, had given it everything, and had fallen just short. When the final whistle went, I hugged Mam, and we hung around for a spell to watch the celebrations on the field. The rain started then, and we went for cover on the concourse. Paul and Enda were seated not too far from us, and they joined us in short order. No one was too upset, but a late free given to Kerry against Galway centre-back John Daly for overcarrying was the focal point around which our disappointment would be focused.

Within a couple of minutes we were able to find video of the incident online. It might not have been a free in, but it wasn't a free out either. It was harsh, but a four-point winning margin brooks no argument. As long as we were inside the walls of Croke Park, it felt like the game was a going concern. The moment we walked out, it hit us – that was it. Kerry were All-Ireland champions.

Mam and Dad headed off to Glasnevin again, taking their time on the walk back. Brian and Adam slipped away as well. Paul, Enda, Connolly and I started walking down the North Circular. I was eager to go for a pint, just to prolong the day, but the boys wanted to hit the road. I could hardly blame them.

Mark Horgan had managed to wangle a ticket to the match for himself, and he was on his bike meeting our friend Clare after the match. They were touring the northside, looking for somewhere to have a drink, and ended up in Pantibar on Capel Street. And so it was that my first real debrief of the All-Ireland final happened in Ireland's most famous LGBTI bar, getting served an insanely nice pint of Guinness by the most beautiful Brazilian girl I'd ever seen.

Mark and Clare were quietly devastated on my behalf. They were, in fact, so upset for me that it nearly broke my heart – evidence, if evidence were needed, that my friends are aware of the extent to which this nonsense takes up so much of my life. I had earlier left my suit in Clare's house, as I was going to Galway's post-match banquet as a guest of Connolly's younger brother the stats-man, and as I had a sneaky second pint I considered blowing off the banquet altogether to drown my sorrows with my GAA-agnostic friends. But duty called, and I would be going with Flesk, who was always entertaining, even at a sports funeral. I went back to Clare's house with her, changed into my suit and headed to Ballsbridge.

Flesk arrived soon after and we wandered up to the hotel bar. We had been told that the event was strictly for the friends and family of the team, and so I had horrible visions of myself and Flesk sticking out like two sore thumbs. But there must have been 400 people there or more, and it was full of Milltown people. I saw lads I hadn't seen in years, and it was a brilliant night, in its way. Everyone there was having a good time, while also speculating inwardly on just how much better it would have been if Galway had won the shagging thing. I didn't stay too long, as I knew I had work in the morning, and an All-Ireland final to try to dissect as objectively as possible . . . but as we were leaving, John Daly came over to us. He knew Flesk well through work, and he also remembered the *Second Captains* TV show, which I'd assumed he'd have been too young to recall.

As he was talking to me about that, I was just staring mutely at him. I couldn't help myself. 'What the hell was going on with that free at the end – what a load of bollocks.' It was out of my mouth before I'd even thought about it. I'd said the same thing to pretty much everyone else I'd met that night, and now I was saying it to the man who had actually had the free given against him . . . knowing full well that he'd be hearing little else for the next three weeks.

I didn't even have drink to blame. It was time for home.

13. Our Place Against Your Place

The last senior championship game I started for Milltown was against Salthill-Knocknacarra in July of 2009. It featured five red cards, and I got one of them.

The first three were a direct result of a brawl that involved at least sixteen players. I was involved in a peripheral, 'Please, Lord God, not the face' kind of way, pulling a few of our lads away from the scene of the crime, pushing a few opponents, but certainly not as an arch-combatant. The game had barely settled down when I picked up a second yellow card for a foul that in the normal run of events might have been glossed over, but which was a perfect opportunity for the referee to even up the score after Salthill had lost two men to our one in the melee. I gave him the chance, and could have no complaints.

It was the only red card I've ever received in my life and, given the circumstances – we only lost the game by a couple of points, having had a third man sent off in the second half – it was a fairly depressing dressing room afterwards. This was compounded by the fact that, when I emerged from that dressing room, I found out Mam had fallen walking down the steps out of Tuam Stadium and broken her arm. It fairly put the tin hat on the day.

I was still working on *Off the Ball* at the time, and a mass brawl in a county championship game with five red cards was certainly newsworthy enough to appear on the radar of our listeners. Barely twenty-four hours after it had happened,

I was on national radio answering texted queries about my disciplinary record.

The way that story got onto the radar of the national media was indicative of how violence in the GAA gets covered. The match report will appear, with the usual descriptors attached, carrying the names of the players dismissed. The ensuing coverage will have much more to do with the presence or absence of a good photographer, or videographer, at the game than the ferocity of the exchanges.

There were no pictures of our brawl against Salthill, so it didn't go any further. Also, the game was played in July, so there was plenty of other GAA news coming in from around the country. The landscape is rather different in late September or October, when newspapers are much more willing to have a big splash on a row, again provided there are some photos of it all.

The number of games that were played out in front of cameras went up dramatically as a result of the pandemic, and, of course, everyone with a smartphone is now a content producer as well, so while it might seem like violent episodes are on the rise in the GAA, the truth is somewhat more nuanced. Not that that should be a source of reassurance for anyone. This has been going on for ever; we're just actually able to look at more of it now.

To a journalist on a live radio show, it was an extraordinarily frustrating type of story to cover. The only comment you'd ever get on the record was that the county board would investigate the brawl as a matter of urgency. Then the reaction boils down to shrill condemnation and agreement that, yes – this is bad; and, no – we have no idea how to stop it from happening again.

Years later, in October 2021, when writing my column for

the *Irish Times*, I was presented with the image of an under-15 game from Wicklow between Kilcoole and Carnew descending into a massive brawl involving players, mentors and supporters. A clip of the scrap captured on someone's phone garnered over a million views in a couple of days.

There were a couple of aspects of that particular incident that made it especially infuriating to me. First of all, the mere fact that you're dealing with fifteen-year-old boys, and their mentors who really should know better, creates a grim prospect for the next twenty years of those young boys' football careers. One of the mentors to the fore in the fisticuffs was wearing a 'give respect, get respect' bib and, as I noted at the time, he really didn't need to engage in much navel-gazing: a mere glance downward should have been enough.

You always hope that the incident you're reading about – and, let's be clear, there's never any shortage of these to choose from – will be a turning point. But there have been enough incidents that looked like potential turning points in the past to suggest that what we're actually doing is going around in circles. County board investigations always boil down to a case of trying to identify individuals, issuing bans to spectators that will be almost impossible to enforce, and a general feeling that, while individuals are punished and the association suffers reputational damage, nothing really will have been learned or gained from the whole experience.

One detail that jumped out from the subsequent reports of that Wicklow under-15 final was that, after tempers had cooled, there was a cup presentation attended by mentors, supporters and players of both teams that went off without further incident. I was trying to figure out why I was so annoyed by that detail, and I think it was because it spoke to something central to all this: the distinguishing lines between the players on the pitch, the coaches on the sideline, and the fans behind the wire are always far too blurred when it comes to the GAA. It's laughable to think that managing to get through a cup presentation minutes after exchanging punches and kicks with a bunch of strangers was something for these adults to be proud of, a sign of respect and honour restored.

A football match, whether between the Kilcoole and Carnew under-15s or any other two clubs, is never just a contest between two sets of players. It's always 'our place' against 'your place', with all the attendant bluster that brings. Players shaking hands at the end of a hard-fought game is a pretty basic component of competition at any level. The mentors can do that too if they're so inclined, and the fans are free to mingle or stick to their own as they please on the sideline. But magnanimous post-game shows of sportsmanship are for the players to exchange. If you're a supporter, then for God's sake just stay off the field.

There appears to be no mental separation between players, mentors and supporters. The players should play, the coaches should coach, and fans should stay the hell out of it until the game is over and you console or congratulate your own. It might be 'your place' playing 'their place', but the honour of the little village is not at stake. That's the bit we struggle with. If you're wearing a bib, or a pair of loafers, you're a non-combatant; both metaphorically and, it seems necessary to point out, literally.

The Galway–Armagh All-Ireland quarter-final in 2022 featured an eye-gouge by a member of Armagh's extended panel, Tiernan Kelly, on Galway's Damien Comer at the end of normal time. It was caught on camera, there was no argument, and Armagh and Kelly accepted his twenty-four-week ban without complaint. But even in a situation like that you will find people eager to play it down, as if to say that, apart from the eye-gouge, it wasn't actually too bad. ('Aside from that, Mrs Lincoln, how did you enjoy the play?')

People who make such arguments sometimes point at fractious rugby games, that might feature twelve- or fourteen-man bouts of pushing and shoving. The key difference is that any row in a rugby game almost always takes place inside the white lines, and *between the players*. There are no substitutes racing eighty yards to get involved; no members of the extended panel racing across the pitch in their civvies. Management aren't pulling their players apart in the middle of it. Running onto the field to get involved in an incident that doesn't concern you is practically unheard of in rugby.

In the GAA there is a refusal to see a row as anything other than an event on which the reputation of the village (or the county) depends. That's why mentors, substitutes, non-togging substitutes and fans get involved, and turn an on-field scrap into a glorified faction-fight.

The rule book has proved unfit for the task of stopping this from happening regularly. The people at the front line, the referees, have it all to do just to protect themselves.

A sports psychologist at Ulster University, Dr Noel Brick, and three colleagues sent a survey to over 1,500 GAA referees around the country between February and May of 2022. Responses came in from 438 of them. Among the respondents, 94 per cent said they had experienced verbal abuse at some stage in their careers, and 23 per cent had been on the receiving end of a physical assault. Every time a referee gets assaulted on a GAA pitch – and by 'assaulted' I mean any sort of physical confrontation whatsoever – it should be a national story. But when referees do try to enforce the rules, they are more often than not let down by their county boards.

I have often wondered why these brawls tend to happen more often in football than in hurling. Of course, there are far more football matches than hurling games played every weekend, but the absence of a clearly defined tackle rule in football must be a contributory factor. It breeds frustration on the line and in the crowd. That transmits itself to the pitch. The players get edgier and edgier, and the pot finally boils over.

Barring supporters is an ineffective punishment. For many of these people, the only place where they can be reliably recognized is at their own home ground, which means the only people who can stop them from attending are their own clubmates. If we want to change behaviour, we need to start penalizing clubs.

When I contacted Dr Brick after first reading his report, he told me that verbal abuse leads to physical abuse – one is indisputably connected to the other. If your club continually allows referees to be spoken to in a disrespectful fashion, then you're asking for trouble. Equally, if respect for the referee is bedded in, then people are likelier to respect the white line that separates the players from everyone else.

In the summer of 2022, an assault on a referee in Roscommon left him requiring hospitalization. The individual responsible was banned for ninety-six weeks, but the rule book proved to be no deterrent. Instead of that moment precipitating a reckoning, we saw an epidemic of similar attacks on referees throughout the following weeks.

If the actions of a supporter or a mentor mean players miss out on a year of competitive sport, the system becomes self-regulating. Players won't put up with it because ultimately they will be the ones suffering the consequences.

*

Apart from the unfortunate red card incident against Salthill, the only other row that really sticks out from my own career was among the most surreal occasions I've ever experienced on a football field.

Challenge games in January are never exactly a barrel of laughs, but they come with a sense of relief that at least it's not a heavy physical session. It's also a reminder of why all that training goes on: at some stage in the dim and distant future, a referee will throw in the ball and a football game will happen.

It is January, soon after the beginning of this century, and I am a teenager playing for the Milltown senior team. We have decided in our wisdom to play our near-neighbours Dunmore MacHales in a pre-season challenge. It is miserable, it is wet, and if 90 per cent of the players haven't been out the night before, it is bloody close to 90 per cent.

I jog into my position at corner-forward, where I am met by the same fella who always plays corner-back for Dunmore. This is a strange relationship in its own right: the connection that grows between you and the corner-back you've marked dozens of times. The two of you might have barely exchanged a word with each other, but you feel a kinship of some kind nevertheless.

With the lads you've done well against, there exists a great convivial bond. 'This guy is a lovely fella, leaving football aside entirely – I'd like to have a pint with this lad some day, really just chew the fat, get to know each other.' The lad who has cleaned you a couple of times is naturally a bad egg, a wrong 'un, a disreputable character. 'I respect him as a footballer, but I want nothing to do with him as a man.'

The Dunmore corner-back and I politely discuss what we got up to the night before – we may even have been in the same drinking emporium. (This was a time in my life when

PJ's Nite Club in Dunmore was a central part of my weekends – and yes, the house DJ was known as DJ PJ.)

The game begins at a torpid, almost comatose pace. It is clear that this will be the most pre-seasonish of pre-season challenge games. After a number of minutes, however, some confusion is building. One of the Dunmore midfielders has refused to take off his tracksuit top. It's pretty much the exact same shade of green as his teammates' jerseys, but our midfielder is not amused. Apparently our man believes that the wearing of a tracksuit top demeans the entire fixture. Some jawing ensues. Moments later, our man tries to rip the tracksuit top off his opponent. All hell breaks loose. What had started as an early season loosener has now assumed all the deadly seriousness of a championship Sunday.

Blows are exchanged, bitter words too. I feel sufficiently distant from the main table of events to suggest to my Dunmore opponent that we negotiate a side treaty. I have no quarrel with you, John. This is a drama currently being played out far from our field of influence (over sixty yards, at least). If we stick together, we might just see the end of this war.

The game ends, and I make hesitant inquiries: was there some previous incident that could have sparked this day's conflict between our man and their man? It emerges that they used to play rugby together. They are close friends. There will be no further explanation forthcoming, apart from the wider, too-wide-for-the-naked-eye-to-see explanation, which is that we're all fucking insane to begin with.

14. Lions in Winter

I had played for Templeogue Synge Street's second team for two years in Division 5 of the Dublin adult leagues when, at the start of 2019, it emerged that Denis Bastick, a five-time All-Ireland winner, was going to be joining our squad for the coming year. I had just been appointed team captain, and immediately started planning my victory speeches. He was obviously going to transform our chances.

In our first league game, which was my first time as captain of anything since an under-21 game for Milltown in 2002, I played wretchedly. We got a free forty-five yards out late on, and Bassy calmly strolled across, stroked it over the bar, and won two league points for us that we scarcely deserved. I felt like one of those Kilkenny captains who had been put forward by their club but couldn't make the starting championship team. It didn't matter who the captain was: this was going to be Bassy's team.

But it didn't quite work out like that, because Denis's body didn't allow him to finish out his inter-county career and enjoy his club football for the three or four years that he'd obviously hoped to spend with the lads he'd grown up with. He retired from Dublin at the end of the 2017 season. He played with the Synger senior team in 2018, but never got a clear run of fitness. Two of his best mates were on the team that I was on, so he dropped down to us in 2019, and I'm sure hoped to find down there a level of football that would be physically less taxing. But every time he took his socks off and allowed us a look at his ankles was a reminder that he had pushed himself far beyond the limits of a regular person. They were swollen up like fists, lumps of gristly muscle and bone that made you wince.

He played a few games for us, and made huge contributions every time. He spoke brilliantly in the group, and we learned so much from him. But he never got a clear run of three or four weeks where he could train and play without pain, and it was a different contribution from the one he had hoped to make.

It was interesting to watch opposing teams reacting to the sight of a Dublin inter-county legend lining out for us. As I walked into position, I'd see my opponent straining his eyes looking out to midfield, his heart sinking: 'Is that . . . is that Denis Bastick?' And then, as Bassy struggled to last a half, there would be that moment when the man marking him would stick his chest out and start thinking to himself, 'Jaysis, this Bastick fella isn't that great' – as if the player he was marking was the same footballer who turned the game and set up the decisive goal of the 2013 All-Ireland final against Mayo.

Many, many years before that, in 2001 or 2002, I was in Kenny Park in Athenry watching Joe Cooney playing a club championship game for his club, Sarsfields. He was probably thirty-six or thirty-seven, had long retired from inter-county hurling, and was playing with a club team that was on a slow, inexorable slide from the heights of winning back-to-back All-Ireland club finals in 1993 and 1994.

It was a beautiful summer's evening. Cooney lined out at midfield, and he was quietly, defiantly magisterial. The legs had gone, there was no doubt about that, and all he had left was the box of tricks that he had used to such effect throughout possibly the most decorated hurling career a Galway man had ever had. But that box of tricks was extensive, and he emptied it that evening. It was an extraordinary performance, and that game has stayed in my mind as possibly the perfect distillation of the GAA lion in winter.

There have been many words expended on the topic of sports stars struggling to adjust to civilian life after years in the spotlight of top-level sport. I've talked to former Dublin player and GPA chief executive Paul Flynn about that transition, and he told me about an NFL players' union representative he'd once invited over to Ireland from the US who'd told him that, in professional sport, retirement was jumping off the edge of the cliff, whereas playing for your GAA club could be more positively described as an off-ramp.

But it's been a little sad to see how so many of the players from that great Dublin team of the past ten years are too beaten up to contribute to their clubs in the way that they'd like. One of Templeogue Synge Street's other decorated Dubs, Eoghan O'Gara, played a big role for the club even after his Dublin retirement, but there are others, like Paddy Andrews, Cian O'Sullivan, Michael Darragh MacAuley, and more, who didn't really get that chance.

Inter-county players sometimes talk of wanting to 'give back' to their clubs. In truth, they've already given too much. GAA people sometimes even speak of a 'debt'. What do all these phrases actually mean? The club were lucky to have an exceptional player come through their underage ranks, they won plenty of juvenile games on the back of the quality of that player, and then he or she went on to bigger and better things with their inter-county team, all while returning in the autumn to play the club's most important games throughout the peak years of their careers. To the outside world, ten years of juggling county and club playing is an exceptional effort. But to the GAA man or woman, the bill is not yet paid.

I think there is, deep in the heart of many GAA people, a desire to see the inter-county player fade in front of their eyes – a fetishization of suffering. It's the only way they'll know the player has given it their all. This may help explain why so many fine inter-county players hang on (and are kept on) for too long with their counties – and why it's rare for players to retire when still near the peak of their powers, as Joe Canning, Michael Murphy, and Lee Keegan so admirably did.

The answer seems simple. If a player is really desperate to be in a position to contribute to their club after their best days are behind them, then they retire from inter-county at thirty-three, rather than at thirty-five or thirty-six. Of course, that isn't quite as simple as it sounds. Trying to stay on the inter-county hamster-wheel, even when getting little game-time, is infinitely more testing on the body than the rhythms of a club season. But players in that position seem to develop a kind of Stockholm syndrome. They're not enjoying their sport, they're not getting picked, but they still don't quite know how to say goodbye to it all. And who could blame them? Many of them have forsaken the friendships that got them through their teenage years, have drifted away from their clubmates, have eschewed work nights out to prioritize training and playing at a maniacal standard. And their closest friends are in that inter-county bubble. They're not just walking out on top-level sport, they're also walking out on the only social peer group they've known for a decade.

They piss and moan about their lack of inter-county game-time, but they can't bite the bullet and make a decision – when a return to club football would give them all the football they could handle. Meanwhile, their body is breaking down more and more with each doomed attempt to get back up to speed. When such players do eventually return to their clubs, they are likely to be a husk of the player they were.

I was talking recently to a physio who used to work in rugby. She told me that provincial rugby players get a year's extra free physio treatment after the end of their careers. This seems to be the least county boards could do for players who have played more than, say, five years at inter-county level. The GPA has tried in the past to incorporate a free medical screening for every player after they've retired, to diagnose lingering injuries and ensure that they got the treatment they deserved for injuries incurred while a county player, even if they were stepping away from the top level.

While the physical toll is undeniable to anyone who's seen it at first hand, there is still a cultural lag in how it's viewed by the public. A county man who doesn't go back and dig in for his club for a couple of years in his mid- to late thirties is not looked on very favourably, regardless of what state his body is in. If he was fit to play in an All-Ireland final last year, the question will be asked why he can't be fit to play for his club for a couple of months the following summer.

The chance to do that is not something given to every player. But some members of the Dublin team of the last fifteen years have done it brilliantly. Tomás Quinn was pulling strings for the St Vincent's seniors into his forties, still a massively important player on one of Dublin's marquee teams. Rory O'Carroll was better than he'd ever been for Kilmacud Crokes in 2021 and 2022, well after he'd left Dublin behind him.

Dan Shanahan retired from inter-county hurling at the age of thirty-three, and his post-Waterford hurling career was as admirable as anyone's, but the last chapter of his story illustrates the potential pitfalls as well. In September 2022, he retired from club hurling after playing his thirtieth season of senior championship for Lismore. It demonstrated the most extraordinary dedication to the cause.

His final game ended up being on live national television, Lismore's quarter-final defeat to Mount Sion. He was taken off at half-time, in a game where Lismore were comprehensively outclassed. That wasn't the ending he deserved, but it is the ending that all great inter-county players risk when they continue to play for their club long after the gifts that took them to the top of their sport have waned.

I feel it myself as an auld stager, even playing at my modest level. My fear every day is that today will be the day that I meet a fella who is just too good, too young, too strong – a fella who'll go through me for a short-cut, and comprehensively end any thought I might have of continuing to compete at this level. Ensuring that today won't be that day is, in many ways, the main motivating factor every time I play a game.

Now imagine what it's like when you've known the experience of having Croke Park in the palm of your hand, of winning All-Stars and All-Irelands . . . and suddenly you're in the middle of a game you expect to dominate, with fifty people watching, and you're being handed your arse by some young lad with a point to prove. That must be a devastating moment for any inter-county player. And that's the tightrope anyone walks every time they play past their prime.

Within the GAA, the decision of whether or not to play on is not really seen as the player's own. The club will say, 'We know you're not at your best, but you're still better than what we have, so we need you.' And instead of walking away when you're no longer the dominant player on the team, you're asked to change focus and consider whether you can be a help to the team in any way. If there's a role for you at full-forward, or as a sweeper, or as an impact substitute.

If you're on board, then this can probably be a weirdly freeing moment, but that still doesn't mean that you don't risk personal pride every time you go out there. When Dan Shanahan was taken off at half-time in that game against Mount Sion in 2022, there will have been people (and I know, I heard from a few of them) who would say that it was a fairly bad look for a club like Lismore to be playing a forty-five-year-old, and that Dan would have been as well off calling a halt a few years ago instead of taking a spot from some young fella.

It doesn't matter to these people that Dan was merely answering a call from the club management after a spate of injuries earlier that summer, or, indeed, that if there was a young fella good enough to take his place, he'd be playing already. Even as the star man's ego is being bruised, that ego stands accused of convincing him he's still capable of working miracles.

If this all sounds rather bleak, playing for your club can also provide a long, distinguished career with a perfect send-off. The 2021 Leitrim county final was the first ever shown on national television, and anyone who watched that day was given a front-row seat to an exceptional performance from Ballinamore Sean O'Heslin's veteran wing-back Wayne McKeon.

He kicked five points, most of them absolute peaches, and he spent almost the entire afternoon bombing outside-of-the-boot passes forty or fifty yards downfield. Every touch he had was designed to be decisive. He kicked more contestable passes in one sixty-minute period than most footballers do in an entire championship run, so his possession stats might not have made for great reading, but he broke the game open time and time again.

He showed the leadership, the willingness to make mistakes, and the big-game temperament that is often something only your county man, past or present, can offer. And sometimes everything you have is enough, even when that everything is a long way off your all-time best.

15. What You'd Rather Do

On the morning of a Galway Senior Football Championship quarter-final a number of years ago, I woke up somewhere in a field at Goodwood Racecourse near Chichester, in the south of England. Gillian was teaching in England at the time, and the music festival at Goodwood was supposed to have been the end-point of a week-long break for the two of us in London. I'd had to back out of the London trip for work reasons, but the music festival at the weekend was a non-negotiable, as would be made clear to me.

The game in question, to be played in Tuam Stadium, had been fixed for that Sunday with grim inevitability a couple of days after our win in the previous round, which had seen me come on at half-time and somehow kick four points, having not really played a whole pile that year. That, it turned out, was my first and biggest mistake. Prior to that, my absence for the next round would have been greeted with a shrug roughly in keeping with the diminution of my abilities by that time. Instead, all of a sudden, I was seen as reasonably useful again.

In a move familiar to most GAA players, I kept my head down and prayed for some deus ex machina to appear and solve all my problems. When that didn't materialize, I approached Gillian with a suggestion that I perhaps skip the festival. The idea was not met with great enthusiasm. In fact, no enthusiasm whatsoever. I could perhaps go even further and say Gill's counter-suggestion involved some body parts (mine) being lopped off by a non-expert in the field (her), with no anaesthetic.

The compromise, when it came, was that I would go to the festival on Friday and Saturday and then depart, refreshed and ready for action, at 7 a.m. on the Sunday (leaving Gill alone in a tent she'd have to take down and carry home herself). And so I found myself walking to a train station (wearing a vintage Royal Navy coat that I had bought at the festival and thought was cool but which I also knew I would never wear again after that day) en route to Gatwick Airport as the early morning fog drifted over the Sussex Downs.

I had not had much to drink the night before, maybe three gin and tonics, but even as I was drinking them I realized the full stupidity of the situation I found myself in. If the gin and tonics don't get you, Murph, the sleeping-bag, the tent, the two flights, the tiredness, and the terrible nutritional intake of the previous days probably will.

It was the early 2010s, and Galway Airport was still operating at the time, so I could change planes at Dublin and take a second flight to Galway. I walked from one gate to the other, and took my seat waiting for the Aer Arann plane to arrive. It appeared likely that I would be the only person on it until two figures approached the gate just as the flight was about to start boarding. Two very recognizable figures. Two unmistakable figures. I would be taking this Dublin–Galway journey with Jedward, and no one else. This seemed very much in keeping with the general tenor of my day.

Mam and Dad picked me up at Galway Airport and I went home for some dinner before the evening throw-in at Tuam Stadium. I remember feeling pretty tired but also as if I might have gotten away with it somehow. Not from the point of view of management, who knew that I was flying home for the game (if not about Jedward), but from my own perspective. I actually didn't feel that bad.

You can convince yourself of many things, but that doesn't make them true. I knew I wasn't going to start (a detail I'd decided to spare Gill), but when I was called on with fifteen minutes to go we were in a tough spot, and I was in no shape to turn the game around. We were well beaten, and I walked out of Tuam Stadium knowing that this couldn't go on for too much longer.

So. Two flights, ruining your holiday plans, risking your relationship, to come off the bench in a game you knew you weren't going to start, and on top of all that knowing that the fact that you'd even had to make the journey back would be used against you as a sign of your wavering commitment. I made the decision to play that weekend knowing all of those things to be true. It was, obviously, utterly insane.

Why?

Really, though – why?

Go on, then, Murphy, try and answer the question you've been asked a million times.

You love your club, of course. And love is certainly one emotion that you could ascribe to the motivations club players have for doing what they do every summer. But there are other emotions, less noble than love. Perhaps the biggest one is guilt. Then there's a desire to be liked, a wish to conform with your peers.

The guilt can be traced back to the effects of playing and training with a group of people roughly your own age over a period of years. In that atmosphere you depend on the lads who are good at defending to defend, the fit lads to do the running, and the accurate players to score enough to win the game. It is Henry Ford's assembly line, and if you have a part to play, you know your absence impacts those working either side of you. Maybe your contribution is minimal, but it's there. It's part of the machine. And the absence of it creates a problem.

You want to be liked. You want to be known as someone people can depend upon, selfless in pursuit of a collective goal, i.e. a county title. But let's focus on love. Because while I definitely went through phases of not liking Milltown GAA club's impact on my life, I have to say that I never stopped loving the club itself.

I love it because it's a link to my parents and to my childhood and to my home. The thing that makes me feel most like a Milltown person is the fact that I used to play football for the GAA club, and I still go back to see them play two or three times a year. When (for example) Milltown lads Eoin Mannion and Jack Kirrane won those All-Ireland under-20 medals with Galway in 2020, it gave me joy even though I'd never spoken to either of them before.

My mam and dad still live there, obviously, but they don't tie me to Milltown in the same way the GAA club does. If they decided to move to Malaga in the morning, I'd go and see them there. The GAA club is never going to move.

When I joined Templeogue Synge Street in 2017, things were going to be different. I didn't have any spiritual links to this place, I was there to enjoy myself, and so if games were on weekends that didn't suit me, I wouldn't be there. It would be football without the guilt. It would also be football without a deep emotional connection, but that's all right – when did that ever cause me anything but trouble?

You go down training with that mindset, and it reminds you how much fun the game is. You start to make friends. All of a sudden, in your first season, after it's taken you three or four months to even remember how to play, you find a bit of form. You're starting to play well. You qualify for a promotion play-off, and it's fixed for a Sunday morning. And, of course, you're invited to the afters of your best friend's brother's wedding the night before. It's in a beautiful hotel, full of brilliant, talented people who you would love to spend time with . . . and you decide, feck it, I'll just drive there and back and not drink. It saves us trying to find somewhere to stay overnight, it's less hassle, and also there's that nagging feeling in the back of your head. The match. It's what you'd rather do.

It's what you'd rather do.

I went and played that game, and pulled a hamstring inside the first five minutes. But I didn't regret the decision. Because after leaving behind that feeling of being wanted, of being part of a team, I realized how much I'd missed it. And while I promptly let the side down by getting injured in record time, I loved it.

So while I spent a good number of years justifying my travelling back and forth to play for Milltown as a sort of grim duty, which I was performing solely so my father would not be getting grilled by fellas in Mullarkey's, my time with Synger has clarified my thinking. I love the game, and I love being part of a team, and my ego loves the idea that I am still useful to a team.

Fast forward another three years, and my closest friends have hired out Galley Head Lighthouse in West Cork for a weekend away. They'll be down there for three days, eating food that they've cooked themselves, going for walks, pints in Clonakilty – in the normal run of events, this is my favourite way to spend a weekend. But there's a county quarter-final against Raheny fixed for the Saturday, and there's no way I'm missing it. I'm the team captain, what the hell else am I going to do? Again – it's what I'd rather be doing.

I miss a penalty in the first half, I score two penalties in the second half, I fist a score wide when I should have played it square to a teammate for a goal that might have got us back in the game, and I spend about six months regretting that decision not to pass that ball. The missed weekend away never even registers on the regretometer.

Only one of the eight other people who were due to go on that weekend away played GAA, and that at a reasonably modest level. The rest of them work in law, or in the arts, or are recovering unionists. None of them care about the GAA in any real way. They're not morally opposed to it, they're not rugby or soccer fans with an axe to grind, they just . . . don't get it. They're fascinated up to a point by my willingness to miss things for it, but obviously that fascination has its limits too.

'You like it, and that's good. We're happy for you. But jeez, spending time with your friends is also fun, no? And I personally don't feel like being press-ganged into being anywhere at any time by anyone who isn't paying me a wage.' Their (and her) attitude was succinctly described by Gillian as 'general bewilderment'.

And yet – it's what I'd rather do. It's infuriating to me to even admit that.

I'm glad that most of my best friends don't care about the GAA. In fact, I'd say it's the most important factor in the maintenance of my sanity. It gives me a perspective on the entire landscape that I don't think enough GAA members get.

Gillian doesn't care either, but she's necessarily more

involved in it all. When we first met, I wasn't playing any football at all – she maintains I suckered her in under false pretences. When I returned to play for Milltown, she was working in a retail job, which meant we basically never saw each other for the length of the football season. That certainly didn't endear the GAA to her.

But since I joined Templeogue Synge Street, she's been an enthusiastic supporter of my football career . . . or, at least, of my spending a large portion of Tuesday and Thursday nights out of the house. She realizes too that this won't go on for ever, that any sort of physical activity is good for a man in his forties to be engaging in. And, let's face it – she sees how much I enjoy it. My smile is so goofy after we win a game that she can't help laughing at how a grown man could care this much.

I love when friends of mine are curious about something and come to me for answers. Gill and I might be in the pub, watching a GAA game on television, and if she sees an American couple glancing up at the TV screen, trying to figure out what they're watching, she knows she might as well go home. All I'm hoping for is one question in my general direction and she knows I'm away. Inside two minutes, the unsuspecting Yanks will have heard about Dick Fitzgerald's coaching manual, the 1947 Polo Grounds Final, Ja Fallon, and Jimmy Barry Murphy.

I went to the 2011 All-Ireland hurling final with my good friend the travel journalist Fionn Davenport, and I loved every minute of it, explaining the minutiae of the game and the occasion to a neophyte. In fact, I think that might be my preferred viewing option for a game that doesn't have as one of its combatants a team I'm deeply emotionally involved in – having someone good-naturedly listening to me as I drone on about the glory and the wonder of it all in the seat beside them. I was sitting beside the well-known soccer journalist Dion Fanning for the 2016 All-Ireland hurling final, and correctly predicted that Tipperary player John O'Dwyer's post-match interview on the field moments after the final whistle would include some distinctly unparliamentary language (I just had a feeling).

Meanwhile, 85 per cent of my conversations with fellow 'GAA people' are spittle-flecked rants of disaffection. The irony is not lost on me. We complain because that is the state of mind that comes most naturally to us, but we don't gate-keep the thing at all. I'm an evangelist for it, in the most benign possible interpretation of that word. And it's also true to say that some of the things I evangelize about, the amateur ethos, the pride of the parish, the volunteer element, have their jagged edges rounded and smoothed over for consumption by my audience. The intricacies of those issues are where the interesting conversations are, but that's not where I gravitate when talking with an outsider. Instead, I tend to talk about effort, suffering, and sacrifice for the cause.

Long ago, the marketers working for the GAA's sponsors started selling back to us this notion of unceasing dedication. Every single ad is exactly the same – effort, sacrifice, glory for the little parish. Volunteers hanging up nets, putting up bunting.

During Covid, the former Mayo footballer David Brady offered on Twitter to ring any elderly Mayo fan who was feeling isolated and alone for a chat about football, his career, anything they wanted. It was a beautiful, simple gesture, done completely off his own bat, which summed Brady up. And then AIB swooped in, piggy-backed on it, made a slickly edited video outlining the good deed that Brady had taken upon himself to do ... and now if you google that story, there in the results will be an AIB video. Maybe you'll ask yourself the question – what came first? The good deed, or the deal with a bank? And already they've gotten what they wanted.

They get their tentacles into everything.

The GAA is an organization that is guided by a small number of core principles, and I feel like I've broken most of them.

If there's a single idea at the emotional centre of the GAA, it's that you play for and represent one club, the club of the place that you were born in. I've played senior club championship football for three different clubs, in two different counties.

Another central plank of the GAA is that you dedicate everything, and make sacrifices, and prioritize the glory of your one club. And through that effort and suffering and pain, you will gain a measure of glory. But living the GAA's core principles is not as easy as talking or writing about them.

I have to admit to myself that I have never wanted to give maximum effort. I have never really wanted to sacrifice things for the GAA. I played at home for a couple of summers when maybe it didn't suit me, but there's no point in making myself out to be a martyr. When I was playing, I gave as much effort as I was comfortable with. When I didn't want to do it, I stopped doing it. The same is true now: I commit the exact amount of time to my football every week that I think is appropriate. And playing football is *fun*. Lots of fun. Being a part of a team is fun. I still miss out on things because of football, but those few negatives are outweighed entirely by the amount of enjoyment I get from the game. Maybe that makes me an unreliable chronicler of this life, but it's true for rather more players than the monolithic ideal of the GAA club man or woman would suggest.

There is a fetishization of suffering in the GAA. Every team that wins anything trained harder than everyone else in the competition. Every winning team simply wanted it more. Every team decided in their own heads that nothing was going to stop them this year, and just manifested victory into existence. It's all patently bollocks.

Maybe the team that respects the idea of giving players space away from the pitch, or of telling lads to step away from training for a week if they're just not feeling it, has the right idea. But that story doesn't really sell with GAA people. When Kerry manager Jack O'Connor spoke after the 2022 All-Ireland football final about how much fun he and his team had all year, it sounded vaguely daft. 'Fun? You had fun? How could you have fun working together towards a cherished goal and the fulfilment of all your young players' dreams?'

I can't get away from the fact that I've had so much fun over the years. None of it has been a penance. Some of it has stung, some defeats live with you for ever, but the wins and the laughs and the teammates . . . it's been a joy. When people ask me 'why?' – 'love' and 'fun' seem like two pretty good answers.

16. 'You bloody love this, don't you?' Diary of a Club Footballer, aged 39¾

I played my first game for Templeogue Synge Street's second team in June of 2017. It took me about six months to remember how the game and my body were supposed to work together, but I had a decent season in 2018, and at the start of 2019 I became the first ever culchie captain of an adult team in the club. We won Division 5 (the top half of junior A) that year, and it was probably the most uncomplicatedly happy season of football I'd ever played.

Our manager left to become club chairman that winter, and all of a sudden we had to find a replacement. The club were struggling badly to find someone interested, and so in desperation I rang an old buddy of mine from my college days in Galway, Ray Gilmartin. I knew he lived in the area, and had a son and daughter training in the club's juvenile academy. I also knew he'd been a really good player in his day, because he trained with us in Milltown on a number of occasions back in 2002 and 2003 to keep his fitness up while he was in Galway midweek and unable to train at home in Leitrim with his club Ballinaglera. I got his number and gave him a call. As I listened to the phone ring, I realized what an utterly daft thing this was to do. I tried to imagine what my own response would have been. But before I could settle on the exact method by which I'd tell someone to piss off if they'd called me with such a proposition, Ray had picked up.

I outlined the scenario, and had basically given up on a positive response by the time I'd gotten to the end of my pitch, when Ray said – 'Yes, I'd be interested. Can you give me a couple of days?' A couple of days? I'd have given him a month. He took the job . . . and then three months later, Covid hit.

The league was a write-off in 2020, but we did get a chance to play a championship as the country slowly reopened through September and October. We got out of our group, only to lose to Raheny in the quarter-finals of the Junior 1 Championship.

The following year, we managed to finish a low-stakes league season (played without promotion or relegation, and with our AFL 4 Division split between north and south Dublin clubs). And this time we went all the way to the Junior 1 Championship final, where Clontarf beat us 0-9 to 0-6 on a bitterly disappointing day in November.

I had played poorly in the county final, and had been taken off with about twenty minutes to go, but getting to the county final had won us promotion to the Intermediate Championship, where the club's first team had been barely fifteen years before, so it had been a really good year and we were absolutely going in the right direction.

I had been subbed before the end in most of the games that year, and I saw the writing on the wall. I was about to turn forty, and your captain should be a guaranteed starter, a fella who's pushing standards. It was neither possible, nor advisable, for me to be doing lengthy endurance runs at my age, but the captaincy made me feel guilty about not doing that. I asked Ray, and his coach – the former Leitrim footballer Adrian O'Flynn, who had played senior with the club for years – to please relieve me of it, and they were happy enough to do that. In fact, my suggestion spared them an awkward conversation. Then they talked about a new role for me off the bench, with reduced minutes but hopefully with an impact, and it had an appeal. I hated being off the pitch while the county final was being decided in the last quarter – I hated it. And I'm going to be forty! This obviously isn't going to go on for ever, but I was eager to see what contribution I could make for 2022.

Wednesday, 5 January
As last year's team captain, I have been texted with a question. When do you think we should go back training for the new season? Given we'd lost a county final on 21 November, my honest answer to this question would probably have been around mid-March, maybe Easter.

What I actually said was – 16 January, maybe? The message came through in the team WhatsApp group two hours after I'd sent that suggestion, to say we'd be back on 25 January. I wondered did I now have to text Ray privately and say that I was upset that he had gone against my express wishes, but that I would get over it? In truth, I could have wept tears of joy over those extra nine days.

Tuesday, 25 January
I have done nothing to prepare myself for this. I mean, less than nothing. Cormac, the only man in our team WhatsApp group older than me, has been messaging me and calling me all month asking me to join him on some runs. I feigned interest in this while I was talking

to him on the phone, and even truly believed myself when I said I'd do it, but then the second I was off the phone to him I realized this was the last thing I wanted to do. I had to level with him, but I sent him a text message so pathetic and grovelling that he just texted me back to tell me that it was all just a hobby, that I should just try and regain some enthusiasm from somewhere, and that he loved me.

Before I head out to training, I get my wife to take a couple of photos of me, which I hope to post to Instagram to tell people I'm still a virile young man, capable of competing with men half my age in my chosen sphere. A little endorphin rush from the internet might be just what this evening needs. She takes them, then I drive to Dolphin Park. I sit in the car looking at these photographs before I put my boots on. Then I delete the photos and swear never to wear such figure-hugging fabrics again.

I get injured in what can only be described as a part of training known as the pre-warm-up. What it feels like is a pulled hamstring. But what it actually is I know all too well. It's my back seizing up, and sending pain out to all corners of my mid-section, in time-honoured fashion. Our coach, Adrian, says, 'It's a long season. And listen, I didn't want to insult anyone, but I was going to suggest you do a yoga session instead tonight.' I would not have been insulted . . . but then again, I also would not have done the yoga session.

Friday, 4 February
Today I go to see my physio/osteopath/witchdoctor. He inflicts forty-five minutes of the most exquisite pain

on me, and this will apparently see me right next week, once I can suffer through the weekend. 'That'll burn for about forty-eight hours, so total rest for the weekend.' The Six Nations starts tomorrow, so total rest is something I can absolutely do.

Sunday, 6 February
First challenge game of the season, and I can barely get out of my car, so togging out is definitely not on the agenda. As I try and watch the game with an analytical eye, I realize that management is probably not something I will ever be that interested in, given I spend the first forty minutes obsessing about the performance of the man in my position, the only position in the field I have any knowledge of playing, and the last twenty minutes playing with another injured teammate's dog.

My successor as captain is named today, and I'm glad that management came up with the same name I'd have come up with if I'd had any input. Sean is going to be a brilliant captain, and I'm glad they didn't pick a culchie. Maybe I'll end up being the only culchie to ever captain a TSS team? We can only dream.

Thursday, 10 February
I try and stretch before training at home – I have to give up after five minutes. My back really is in ribbons. This is going to take a bit of patience.

Sunday, 13 February
Our first game of the league is fixed for today, but the weather is brutal, and it's called off.

Sunday, 20 February

Our second game of the league is fixed for today, but the weather is brutal, and it's called off.

This is what you get when you try and play two league games in February.

Saturday, 26 February

There has been a diary clash. We've been invited to play in the Páidí Ó Sé invitational in Dingle, because our old teammate Danny O'Reilly, the lead singer of the Coronas, spends a good portion of his year down there and has gotten very friendly with a few Gaeltacht footballers.

Unfortunately, today is also the day of my twice-delayed St Jarlath's school reunion. After briefly considering Friday night in Dingle, followed by a hellish four-and-a-half-hour drive to Tuam, calmer heads prevail and I ditch Dingle for the comforts of home.

At the reunion, I realize hardly anyone I've spoken to is still playing. One notable exception is Morven Connolly, who plays for Castleknock. He's a year younger than me, and I ask him if he's with the seconds or the thirds – maybe I'll see him on the field one of these days. 'Fuck you, Murph – I'm the first-choice keeper with the seniors.' Everyone else compliments my longevity, while silently judging me.

Thursday, 3 March

My first evening back training with the group – a month's rest hasn't done anything for my back, so it behoves me to just try and get out there and do what I can. I'm off to a good start as I drive down Sundrive

THIS IS THE LIFE

Road in the direction of Terenure rugby club, where we're doing some training under lights. As I reach Kimmage, I realize I've forgotten my boots. Cue a race back to the house, a race to the huddle, and a race to get my stretching done. This all seems slightly hopeless to me. Young lads are flying around me at high speed. I feel thoroughly depressed.

Sunday, 6 March

I tog out to do the warm-up for our long-delayed first game of the season, against Kilmacud Crokes. After that I settle in to take some stats and give management another try. It is tortuous. We win, 1-10 to 2-6, and even writing the substitution slips leaves me a nervous wreck. The sooner I'm back playing the better.

Sunday, 13 March

Fun this morning with nine others at training. The possibility that I might one day play a football match no longer feels quite so unlikely.

Thursday, 17 March

My body is finally starting to respond. When people ask me what it is that I've changed, I'm tempted to say that I've revolutionized my diet, that a rigorous pre-dawn programme of calisthenics has revitalized me . . . but so far the most impactful change I've made is to sit on the couch without crossing my legs, a frankly ridiculous suggestion from a physio of my acquaintance which nonetheless appears to have made a difference.

There's a full round of fixtures across all grades this weekend, and after training I expect to be told to go and play with the thirds, but management are pleased with the work I've done, and are eager to keep me with the intermediates for now. Maybe next time out I'll run with the thirds, but I should come to St Mark's for our second league game on Sunday. I'm a foolish old man, but this makes me happy.

I'm off to Ardmore for a short hotel break with my wife and her mother, for the latter's birthday. While there, I call in on my relatives in An Rinn. My cousin Éanna asks me if I'm still playing a bit of ball. When I answer in the affirmative, I see that reaction again – his eyes narrow imperceptibly. 'What's wrong at home? Is this what a mid-life crisis looks like?' He catches himself, wishes me well, compliments my longevity. Am I perhaps a little self-conscious about this?

Sunday, 20 March
Back to Dublin for our second league game and it's another win, this time a facile one. We have eight subs, five of whom are used, and the other two are eighteen-year-olds who are sent off to play for the thirds later that day. Under no circumstances did I expect to get some minutes, but it was nice to do a full warm-up, do some talking in the huddle, and try and play my part.

Tuesday, 29 March
I've fallen into a pattern of skipping one training session a week – which, without fail so far, has been the training session when the squad have embarked on high-intensity middle-distance runs. My teammates are now convinced I'm in cahoots with management, but

the truth is that I appear to have a sixth sense for when hard physical training is to be done. I can't train tonight, due to work, so I ring Ray, and he dutifully informs me that I will be missing some 800m runs. 'That's unfortunate, Ray, but also unavoidable. Give my love to the boys.'

Thursday, 31 March
Training tonight, feeling old, slightly decrepit, and more than a little surplus to requirements. This is not going too well.

Saturday, 2 April
It's our third league game of the season, against our old rivals Raheny, and I get the last ten minutes, kick a point, take a mark (then unforgivably miss the kick to ruin the good work that preceded it), but suddenly feel like maybe I've got something to offer. Swings and roundabouts, etc. We go out for a few pints. One player asks if any of the management are coming out. I say, 'No,' and he says, 'Yeah, you're a bit of a border-line case though really, aren't you?' As long as I'm missing all the running sessions, they refuse to believe I'm not in cahoots.

Tuesday, 5 April
Best training session of the year, where I found a rhythm in my kicking and couldn't miss for about twenty minutes. Walk off the pitch with the compliments of my teammates ringing in my ears, like a dog heading triumphantly to her favourite corner of the garden to take a piss at her ease.

Thursday, 7 April

Finally, I'm togged out on an evening where some hard running is required. I accept this with the humble good grace with which my teammates are now accustomed, and by that I mean I pass at breakneck speed through the five stages of grief.

Five 600m runs, all to be done in under two minutes, with breaks of three minutes or so between each. I do the first two, the third I get two-thirds of the way through, the fourth I blow off entirely, before I return in triumph to finish dead-last in the fifth. I'm not around the place to run laps, I tell myself. It feels . . . well, hardly good, but at least I'm a participant in the group torture.

Friday, 8 April

I have to get up at 8.30 a.m. to record a piece for our podcast. I'd like to think the scene as I hobble the two yards from my bed to the desk I record from at home is eerily reminiscent of the moment in James Brown concerts when he's led away from the microphone, utterly spent, with a cape sympathetically wrapped around him. Last night's efforts have taken their toll.

Monday, 11 April

I was training yesterday on a beautiful Sunday morning, moving reasonably well, and then out of nowhere – I wasn't even attempting to turn or jink or shoot – my back went. I felt it straight away, walked off immediately, and have had twenty-four hours of really quite excruciating pain. But there's just something about your back going that makes this objectively hilarious. Not for me, obviously, but for everyone else. It's just the archetypal old man's injury.

I haven't told my brothers or parents about my latest bout of back pain, and I haven't told those few remaining friends who ask any more about my football career . . . because I'm a little embarrassed, truth be told. I want to be able to talk to them about my return in triumph. I got a prescription today for some Valium to help me sleep, and some extremely powerful anti-inflammatories. The Valium is a godsend, to be honest.

Saturday, 16 April
My back is actually starting to loosen out a bit. I'm going to Seville for five days next week, our next game is at the end of that week, the same day as Galway and Mayo in Castlebar. If I haven't trained in two weeks, I won't be considered for selection, so even if my back feels better, I'm going to go to Castlebar. I'll see how my holidays agree with me.

Sunday, 24 April
My back felt pretty good at the start of my holiday, but it didn't get a whole pile better while I was in Spain, so I don't need to feel guilty about not being around for the game this morning. The day begins with the news that we've suffered our first loss of the year, 1-11 to 1-5, to Lucan Sarsfields. Our attack was pretty blunt, by all accounts, and while the defeat is a sore one, this one detail gives me pause.

Tuesday, 26 April

Went back to training tonight, and my back felt pretty good – I was minding myself, but I got the impression that I might have been in the mix for a start on Thursday in a challenge game against Ringsend ... but, wouldn't you know it, I'm going to a wedding in Mayo on Thursday. There was a level of frustration there as I was walking off, having done OK, but as I write this now two hours after training, I can't help but feel that this is a course correction in my life priorities. In the last three years, when I was team captain, I probably just would've said no to the idea of attending a wedding on a Thursday. Is this what 'getting some sense into my thick head' feels like?

Monday, 2 May

No training all weekend, and I actually would've liked to train on Saturday, just to run some of the alcohol out of my system (the wedding was exceedingly boozy). As it is, we're training at 6.30 on a bank holiday Monday, and it's a fairly light session as we have games on Wednesday and Saturday this week. So no time to make an impact or anything, and even at that I'm not too sharp.

Wednesday, 4 May

Rotten mood all day today. I wrote what I thought was just a so-so column ahead of my 3 p.m. deadline for the *Irish Times*, I was cranky about bills I had forgotten to pay, and I felt myself edging towards an argument with my wife over something truly, cosmically trivial. The game wasn't starting until 8.15 p.m. and the day seemed to stretch out interminably. At 6 p.m. it felt like I'd been waiting all day for a game I definitely wasn't going to start and probably wouldn't feature in. Obviously it was that feeling of complete irrelevance to the team that was fuelling my rather foul humour. An hour in post-work traffic getting across to Clontarf's pitch hardly improved my mood.

And then, you enter a dressing room, and your head clears a little. You're here sharing a common purpose, so get your boots on, get your stretching done, lift your chin. I've incorporated some band work to loosen out my lower back and my glutes, and it's helped me feel better almost immediately. Painkillers have been playing their part recently as well, but I actually feel pretty decent running out to start the team warm-up.

Adrian tells me to take it handy during the warm-up, but to do a fairly intense stretch at half-time, because 'we'll need you in the final quarter'. Hmmm . . . OK! I wasn't sure if I'd see action at all, but this is good. All of a sudden, I'm togged out, I'm here playing with my friends, on a glorious evening for football. All is suddenly right with the world.

The game is unbelievably cagey. They have a couple of lads lying deep in front of our full-forward line, which makes it a nightmare to try and get on the ball. I sympathize entirely with the boys currently in those positions. This is definitely a day to be on the bench rather than starting. We get drawn into a game of patience with them, and we're coming off second-best. I'm brought on with fifteen minutes to go, when we're 6–3 down.

I'm told to go in and try and pick off some points from distance. If I can trundle into a couple of positions just beyond the scoring zone, I might be able to do some damage . . . like an ancient siege-gun, its sights long since warped beyond use, being manoeuvred laboriously into place.

I take my position at the edge of the square, and the first ball that drops into me is hit from distance, with my marker and a sweeper in my vicinity, but it's a beaut. I 'Kenny-Dalglish's-arse' my way into the optimal spot to catch the ball, but it slips through my fingers and breaks free. I just wish I'd had one touch of the ball before trying to make a catch over two lads' heads, but it's gone.

When you're a substitute, you can't hang around, you can't ease yourself into the game. You're sent on to make a difference, so go get on the ball. Given my size, the assumption when I come on is that I'll stand in on top of the keeper and try and scramble a goal, but that's not really what I'm much good at.

The next scenario I find myself in is closer to what I want to do. Our midfielder goes on a burst down the right flank of our attack and is bottled up. This is the run I've made thousands of times – I'm coming on the loop, and get a shot or a pass away before the defence's attention turns from the original ball-carrier to me.

The ball drops to the floor and I manage to get my hands on it. I switch the play immediately to our wing-back, who's about forty yards out directly in front of goal. He's a great kicker of a ball, but I follow my pass and run on another loop around him, fully expecting him to pass me the ball. His shot drops short from maybe thirty-five yards out, and I'm in shock that he's ignored my call for the return and hasn't passed me the ball back.

He was well within his rights to shoot from there, but I think the young folk call this 'main character energy'. On a football field I have major main character energy. I can't conceive that he wouldn't pass me that ball. I say nothing, realizing how unfair it would be to ask for him to pass me a ball when I was only in a marginally more advantageous position, but I'm in the game now.

The next opportunity comes very shortly after. As our attack develops, I can see our full-back joining the attack. When I get on the ball, I know he'll be in space, and I know he won't want to shoot. I give him the ball, and I barely even have to shout for the return. He draws a couple of defenders, and from thirty-five yards out, as I'm moving away to my left, away from goal, I hook a shot up and over just as the defence gets to me.

This is all such a knife-edge. If it goes wide, I'm a substitute trying to make a name for myself, a *mé féiner*. But I know my role: it's to take on the shots that we turned down earlier in the game. I'm happy to accept that there's a high probability of me looking faintly ridiculous taking these shots on, but I can shoot from distance. I might not be able to run, tackle or compete, but I can shoot. And now the deficit is down to two.

They miss a couple of chances, and with maybe two or three minutes left we attack again down our right flank. Diarmuid is a good shooter himself so I position myself wide on the sideline: if he can continue his run, my man won't be in his way. He gets bottled up, and he turns out to Eoin, who is a left-footer like me, so the angle should suit him. He's closed down, so he passes it out to me. The defender who closed him down moves his attention to me, but he's overcommitted to the block, and I dummy-solo inside him. That buys me time, but not enough time to run around and kick it off my instep before the next defender is onto me. So I take the shot on with the outside of my left boot, from twenty-five yards out, about ten yards from the right sideline. It describes an elegant parabola, the ball spinning ever so slightly in the air as it bisects the posts.

The main character energy is now coursing through my veins. I am absolutely certain that if I touch the ball one more time, we'll get a draw. But we don't get another attack. The whistle blows after a couple of Clontarf wides, and we've lost 6–5. It's a bit of a sickener, but we've actually played really well defensively. And despite the low score, this was a genuinely good, highly competitive, intense game of football. There might have been ten people there, but it was a fun game to be a part of.

I walk over to my car, sit in, and reflect on what this is all about. In the moment when the ball flew over the bar for my second point, I could have been any age. This is why I put myself through the pain and embarrassment of the last three months. In that moment it was as though I was saying to my teammates, 'I can still help, I'm not delusional, I'm not deranged, I still have something to offer here.'

It's the start of May, but I also realize that this might not happen again this year – who knows? My body is sore; I don't think it's going to get any better . . . but

I'd still much rather be an influence off the bench at this level than playing sixty minutes at Division 9.

I was so knackered after fifteen minutes of this game that it looks like sixty minutes is beyond me now anyway. So if you're asking me if I prefer to play the first forty minutes, or the last twenty, I think I'm saying the last twenty now. I hate the idea of being taken off just as the game is in the melting-pot. And at that stage the game has opened out a bit, defenders are just a little slower to the tackle – it actually suits me pretty well.

And let's face it – it suits my lifestyle too. I'll be missing a bit of training through work this month, and that would be a big problem if I was trying to make the starting team. But if I'm reasonably well established as an impact sub, then maybe I can tailor my training around my life, rather than the other way around . . .

Saturday, 7 May
At home against St Sylvester's, who are top of the league, we start poorly again, and we're lucky to be only 4–1 down after the opening quarter. At half-time we're 7–4 down. They have a brilliant full-forward who we have failed entirely to tie down. Ken Devine is introduced at half-time, he manages to put the shackles on him, and we find our way into the game.

I get the call to go on a little earlier than on Wednesday night, so with maybe seventeen or eighteen minutes to go – and just as I'm about to run on, we win a free just at the top of the D, slightly to the right of the posts. I run on the pitch with my back to the referee, asking Ray and Adrian on the line if I should take it, they say yes, and before I've even taken my position I've the ball in my hands and about to take a shot.

It goes about a foot wide on the left and I'm furious with myself. It's obviously a free I should have scored, and it was the right thing to take the responsibility on, but it was a weird situation to find myself in, hitting a free with my first touch.

My next shot is an outside-of-the-boot effort that goes wide from way out on the left, and now all of a sudden I'm in that situation I was on the other side of last Wednesday – I look like I'm on here to try and prove a point.

We get another regulation free just to the right of the posts, which settles me, and then we win an even easier free, which I get ridiculously nervous over for some reason. That one goes over, and then we win another free – from a position I'd practised at half-time. It's just over forty-five yards out, but I know exactly how I'm going to hit it, and it starts off right where I want it to. It squeaks just inside the post and now we're right in it, level with a few minutes to go. But it's our starting full-forward Conor Wilde who drags us home, kicking the winner with time almost up. He's been exceptional all evening, and he's developing into a brilliant full-forward, all physicality and pace and direct running.

The full-time whistle is bedlam. Absolute joy. I don't even realize until the warm-down that I roared at my last free from distance to 'GET OVER!', like I was Jordan Spieth. The performance was so good tonight, and I was still able to hit my couple of frees, even if I was sketchy enough.

Tuesday, 10 May

I'm in London for a week with work, so I'm not expecting anything from the next couple of games. I'm just glad I'm back in time to train on Monday evening, before we have two more games in four days. This series of games against good teams is going to define our season.

Wednesday, 18 May

Last week a lad called Ryan Sheehan joined the squad. He's originally from Limerick. It turns out he lives just around the corner from me, so I offer to give him a lift to our game tonight in Naul, against Clann Mhuire. Having been in the situation myself not too long ago, I feel like it's part of my role in the squad to be as welcoming as possible to lads who've joined from country clubs.

He tells me a little about his club at home, Newcastle West. I ask him about the Limerick footballers, who have been having a brilliant year. It turns out he's the brother of Cian Sheehan, who will be playing in the Munster final against Kerry on Sunday week.

I come on again with about twenty minutes to go, and get two simple chances right away that I put over. I can't believe this is how it's working out. I then miss a free with the outside of my boot – an easier free than the one I hit against Sylvester's. Then I drop a relatively simple chance short. Then I get a goal to put us three points up. And then I miss another point from play after having done really well to get into a shooting position.

They win a penalty in the last minute, they equalize and the game's over. I'm sick as a dog. The first half was a total shoot-out – the half-time score was 3-5 to 1-11 – but both teams tightened up massively in the second half, and it was only 1-3 apiece after half-time. It was so low-scoring in the second half that if I'd landed any of the three chances I'd missed, I'm certain we would have won the game.

Saturday, 21 May
We're back up in the north county for a game against Man O' War, another club for whom the team in our division is their first team – which means a bigger crowd, a more uneven spread of ability, and a tense atmosphere. Coupled with the rural setting, it reminds me of playing senior league games with Milltown back in the day.

We're a little short on numbers this evening, down both our regular midfielders, and then one of our replacement midfielders gets sent off after fifteen minutes. Knowing we were short on numbers in the middle of the field, we asked Danny O'Reilly to come out and provide some cover. He has been one of this team's best players for years, a brilliant, all-action mid-fielder, but with the re-emergence of live music this year he had to absent himself from selection to focus on gigging.

Danny's mum is Mary Black, and she's a fantastic supporter of the club. It took a degree of getting used to, the sight of one of Ireland's most legendary musi-cians among a crowd of maybe twenty or thirty people at a league match. In a game in my first year, I went up for a high ball and landed on my neck and head. I was a little shook for a while after that, and jogged rather gingerly back to my position at full-forward. There behind the goal was Mary Black, asking me if I was all right. I thought to myself, either that's a very nice thing for her to do, or this is an extremely realistic concussive hallucination.

There's no sign of Mary at this game in Man O' War, but Danny is back at home in Dublin this week, and we're damn glad to have him because he plays a blinder after being introduced in the reshuffle after the red card.

Even down a man we're in control, but we're missing chances. I'm on again with maybe twenty-five minutes to go, and I end up with 1-3, 0-2 frees, but miss one gilt-edged chance with my right foot. I get my goal with the last kick of the game, we win by four in the end, and I'm just glad the chance I had missed earlier didn't prove to be important.

Sunday, 22 May

I'm back in London with work this Thursday, which means I'm missing training, and if I was fighting for my place I'd be annoyed. As it is, it looks like I'll hardly start a game this year, unless injuries kick in, and I'm guaranteed to come on with plenty of time to make an impact.

When we went down to fourteen last night, I also thought – hmmm, this might not suit me. Maybe this will be the day I don't get on. But I was still brought on in plenty of time, still made an impact, still had the trust of my teammates. I really couldn't be happier. And we're in fourth, in the play-off places with five games to go, so we're right in the mix now.

Wednesday, 1 June

The lack of people at our games is kind of a weird one. I can't exactly blame anyone for not making time to watch their club's second team playing league games in the middle of the week, but it still seems like we should be able to rustle up a few more regular attendees. In fact, our senior team are our best supporters. Lorcan O'Dell and Niall Scully, our two Dublin senior panellists, are actually two of the likelier people to be at our games, and when there aren't too many others, you appreciate it all the more.

My mate Collie decided to come down to the match against Garda this evening. He has no affiliation to TSS at all but he usually comes to two or three of my games a season. As I finish the warm-up and put my sub's bib on, I spot him leaning beside his bike, there for the throw-in. At half-time I stroll over to him and have a chat, tell him I should be on before too long. He's looking at me pretty funny. 'This is a lot more relaxed than I've ever seen you during a football match. The only other time you ever acknowledged my existence was when you got your contact lens knocked out in a game last year, and you barked orders at me and treated me like the home help until I brought it to the attention of your manager.'

And it's true, I don't feel any pressure, even if every game I've come on in has been in the melting-pot when I've been introduced. This one is too, but I get three points from five shots, including a really difficult free from the fourteen-yard line on the sideline, and when it was all over I went back over to Collie. 'You can see why I'm enjoying it so much, right?'

On the hunt for a drinking partner afterwards, I text Ray, who has already poured a glass of white wine for himself at home. We fall to texting back and forth about my role, and I admit to him that as he's reading out the team, I'm still kinda hoping he'll say my name, but that's just muscle memory. How can I complain at the moment? He's honest with me and says I could maybe be starting these games, but who knows what my impact would be over sixty minutes, maybe I wouldn't get to finish many games, and we need scores in the final quarter. I can't say I disagree with a word of that. I head off down to the Royal Oak with Gillian for a pint and I'm as pleased with life as a man of my advancing years can be.

It's a bank holiday weekend coming up, so we won't train again until next Tuesday. Then it'll be three training sessions in a row, Tuesday/Thursday/Saturday, before a game against joint table-toppers Ballymun next Monday. Will my body be fit for it?

Tuesday, 7 June
This was always going to be a running session, with a series of sprints at the end. I line up along the end-line, even though I know it's a bad idea for me to do this, and Adrian has the same thought. He tells me to come over here and practise my shooting.

I'm so happy he did that, and that I didn't just take an executive decision myself to step out after the first three or four. This is management keeping up their end of the bargain. I remain positive about being a sub, they protect my body. They're really a much better management than you've any right to expect at this level.

Saturday, 11 June
We're training at 8.45 on a Saturday morning, and my weekend is now free. Everything is in great shape for Monday evening.

Monday, 13 June
I started the day coughing like a 1950s child with consumption. I came on against Ballymun with twenty to go, after we'd played brilliantly for the first half and led 8–4, but the second half became a complete grueller.

I only touched the ball twice, and felt pretty horrendous throughout. But I kicked a free with my first touch, from about twenty-five yards out, and then with my second touch I kicked possibly the best free of my life, from about forty yards out, five yards from the left touchline. I kept looking for a short one, and then decided fuck this, and bombed it over with the outside of my left foot. It was a hit-and-hope job, but it turned out to be the winner.

The Dublin Masters manager was there to watch my teammate Barry Fitzgerald. Fitzer obviously mentioned my advanced age to him, because he came over to sound out my interest level on the sideline during the first half. I put this into the Murphy family WhatsApp group and got a wide range of responses, ranging from laughter to mild interest in the proposal to outright anger that I could contemplate such a thing. Within minutes my brother Paul (who was born and spent the first four years of his life in Dublin) had sourced the number of the Galway Masters manager and pledged to ring him on my behalf. I think I managed to convince him that would be a bad idea.

Saturday, 18 June

I had been sick as a dog all week, but was starting to feel better and togged out against Cuala. Got twenty minutes, missed a pretty simple chance from play, then missed a really easy free, then missed a tough chance from play. If I'd landed all those, or even two of them, we could have really applied the pressure, but I was nowhere near the level required tonight, and we lost by five.

Cuala are the league leaders, and we could have easily rolled them over. This leaves us a little adrift of the top two, who get promoted automatically, but if you finish third or fourth, you're in a play-off for the third promotion place, so we still have tons to play for.

Wednesday, 29 June

An absolutely brilliant performance from the team against Castleknock, particularly in the first half, just majestic stuff. We won 5-13 to 2-11. Our starting inside-forward line got a goal apiece: they were flying it. I came on for ten minutes at the end and realized that it might have been the first time all year when the result was decided before I got on – and promptly kicked two terrible wides from play. Marty Shovlin, my long-time partner-in-crime in the full-forward line, informed me afterwards that I can only score points when absolutely necessary – so that's my story, and I'm sticking to it.

Thursday, 30 June

We're down to play Skerries Harps at 6.30 p.m. on Saturday, which also happens to be my fortieth birthday. I've been onto Ray for the last three weeks, trying to convince him to get the throw-in put back to 4 or 5 p.m., to give myself a couple of extra hours of drinking. Then word came through early this week that they'd agreed to 5 p.m. Then we found out today that they actually can't field a team, and they've given us a walkover.

Usually walkovers are extremely annoying, but this might be the best-timed one ever given because not only does it give me four extra hours of fortieth-birthday drinking, it also means I can have a few beers at a social evening the club have organized for tomorrow night, which I'm hosting. These events are always better with a few pints on board, and I'm glad I'll be able to enter fully into the spirit of things . . .

Friday, 1 July
The TSS social evening is with Joe Brolly, former Kerry footballer Seán O'Sullivan and Dublin legend Charlie Redmond. Bassy is there as well, and we've a good night – Cormac and Kevin Moran even present me with a birthday cake up on stage.

Wednesday, 13 July
My first game as a forty-year-old, against Ballinteer St John's, and this was my 'Gary Neville at West Brom' moment. So, so bad. I got to start for the first time all year, but I missed frees, I dropped balls, and I felt old. I had travelled back from the West Cork Literary Festival this morning, and I thought I'd done the right thing by breaking up the journey back from Bantry.

Last night I was in Ma Murphys in Bantry after an event, drinking Cokes and spouting opinions about William Faulkner to some writers who knew a lot more about William Faulkner than I did, then sat in the car and drove to Cork city and stayed overnight there. I had to get up and record the podcast this morning, but still felt I'd left enough time to drive home and get rested before the game. But I felt stiff as a board and was just awful.

Having been in a position before tonight where we had a real chance of automatic promotion, we're now struggling to qualify for the play-offs. This was supposed to be the last league game of the year, but we still have one game outstanding from February, against St Vincent's, who are also in the shake-up for promotion. Even a win there doesn't guarantee third or fourth, which would put us in a play-off to become the third promoted team. That final league game against Vincent's won't now be played until after the championship is finished, so we'll just have to park it and try and move on. It'll be there waiting for us once the championship is over.

Realistically, I've now played three bad games in a row, and it's hard to see me having much of an impact for the rest of the year.

Saturday, 16 July

We trained this morning, and in situations like this you have to realize that not everyone is as downbeat about your abilities as a footballer as you can be yourself. I'm lower than a snake's belly, but I still want to keep training, so I keep training. We've three weeks to the first round of group games in the championship, and maybe there can be one more day where I can make an impact off the bench. That's the hope I'm clinging to, regardless of how Wednesday went.

Tuesday, 2 August

We went to a wedding on Sunday, and then to some of the day-two celebrations yesterday. Today I recorded our podcast, tried to write my column and recorded an interview for our RTE Radio 1 show, so I didn't finish work until 6.45 p.m.

After that? Take a painkiller. Stretch for twenty minutes. Go down to the pitch. Stretch for another fifteen minutes. Start training. I'm unable to bend down to pick up balls that are hand-passed to me. Finally, I start to loosen out. We play the seniors for twenty minutes, and I score a goal and a point. All the pain washes away. I'm happy. I'm tired. I'm forty years old. I'm glad for every evening I can do this. I have a bath when I get home. Add the Epsom salts. It's championship this Saturday evening.

Saturday, 6 August

I knew that Conor, our regular full-forward, had picked up a knock, but I still wasn't sure that I'd be trusted to start against St Brigid's. Maybe I care more about how badly that Ballinteer game went than the management do? Anyway, I was named at number 14. I got a couple of decent early touches, then squeaked a poorly hit free just inside the right post for my first point. And after that . . . things just flowed. I ended up with seven points, three from frees, and we won by three.

We went to Devitt's on Camden Street afterwards and I got completely arseholed, told people I loved them, laughed like a drain for four hours. It was a no-holds-barred emotions fest. At one stage, Adrian turned to me and said, 'You bloody love this, don't you?' And it's true, nothing else makes me feel like this. After the Ballinteer game, I just wanted to feel like this one more time. I just wanted to make a difference one more time.

Saturday, 13 August
After a good week's training, this morning is a full-on session, with loads of brilliant work done. We usually only train for seventy-five minutes tops, but just when we all reckon we've gotten to the end, the lads are put through a sort of athletic murder-thon, which I am again mercifully spared.

Friday, 19 August
Our seniors drew with Raheny 3-7 to 1-13 in Parnell Park tonight, and I went over with our centre-back Mark Hayes and a few others. As we walked out, Johnny McMahon told me we're playing a sweeper in our second championship group game against Lucan tomorrow. Who's gonna get dropped?

Saturday, 20 August
For some reason I wake up feeling tired and a bit ragged this morning. My pre-match routine is not set in stone, but today I read for a couple of hours, then go for a coffee and a pastry down the road.

After that, the day is a little like the first chapter of Andre Agassi's autobiography, only instead of non-stop physio and ice-baths as Agassi heroically beats himself into shape to play at the US Open, it's just me, struggling to unload the dishwasher. 'You'll be OK, you'll be OK,' I tell myself . . . I'll loosen out.

I eat at 3 p.m., for a 6 p.m. throw-in. At 4.30, having taken a painkiller and stretched for twenty minutes or so, I feel like my back will be OK. I arrive at Lucan's home ground, and I remind myself that I've always played well out here. We tog out, get onto the field, and for whatever reason I'm just not feeling brilliant. The team is named and I'm starting at full-forward again. We warm up at the far end of the field, with a tricky breeze into our faces and across the pitch from right to left. We decide to play against the breeze in the first half if we win the toss.

I played well the last day, but I feel pressure now: pressure to back it up, pressure to last the sixty minutes. I'd have preferred to be hitting my frees with the breeze in the first half, try and get into a rhythm and then be feeling confident facing the wind in the second half.

The warm-up starts, and it's a humid evening, about twenty degrees. I'm struggling really badly, but I know at this stage that this is not predictive. I've felt bad before hundreds of games in the past, and turned it around once the whistle went. This is the value of being twice the age of some of your teammates, I suppose.

I get on the ball early and set up a chance for our wing-forward. I had it in my head after the last day that I need to touch the ball more times than I did. We were able to video the Brigid's game and, having watched it back, I reckon that I scored seven points having touched the ball seven times in open play. Four shots from play, four scores, one assist for a goal chance, one successful hand-pass, and one unsuccessful hand-pass. Put that with the three frees I also scored, and that was the sum total of my involvement. That's basically the game-plan: no one wants me out in the middle of the field chasing my shadow. And against Brigid's it worked. But I'd still like to be a little more involved than that.

My next involvement is to win a free, from exactly where I was having such trouble in the warm-up. But the wind has shifted and calmed, and I'm able to hold the shot off into the breeze nicely. I score another free a few minutes later, but I'm not seeing too much of the ball as they've dropped a sweeper all the way back in front of me.

In situations like these you have to use your head. The reality is that if I stay directly in front of goal I'm a sitting duck for the sweeper. Judging by how the full-back is communicating with the sweeper, it looks like they've targeted me (which is pretty hilarious, given I've barely started a game all year – I can't help but feel that they think I'm Conor).

I immediately start moving to see if the sweeper is focused more on me or on ensuring we don't get in for a goal. I move all the way out to the right corner-forward position and the full-back and sweeper both come with me. Immediately I realize what's required, and vacate the area entirely. We sweep through for a glut of scores. I'm out of the game completely, but that's the job. As long as Ray and Adrian see what I'm doing, I don't mind.

I also see an opportunity to psych out my marker, who must be at least sixteen or seventeen years younger than me. I keep shouting at my teammates to come running straight through the middle, keep making sure he hears me saying that he's leaving the D completely undefended. I see him start to panic. I see him conversing with the sweeper, see them thinking on the hoof. With the last play of the half, with my words hanging in his ears, I can see him getting more and more frustrated at being stuck in the corner away from his natural position. He cracks, edges into the middle of the defence ten yards to try and make a tackle . . . and Marty spots me out on the wing, draws the full-back to him, pops it over his head, and I'm left with an easy score.

We're 10–6 up at half-time and flying it. We should be further ahead, really, but it was almost the best half of football we've played all year, against a good side. But they switch it up at half-time, ditch their sweeper, press our kick-out, and are much the better team. In the end we're maybe lucky to get out of there with a draw. I get one touch in the entire second half from play, and kick a point. I finish with six points, two from play, and, one missed free aside, it's gone pretty well when the ball's in my vicinity . . . but I'm not exactly conducting the orchestra either, am I?

We go for a few pints afterwards. We end up outside Fallons in the Liberties, the topic of Electric Picnic comes up, and we very quickly realize that six or seven of our starting team are planning on going . . . which happens to be the same weekend as our last championship group game, against Clontarf. A draw will do us, but we may not have a team fit to get us a draw.

Without even thinking, I tell the lads that if they are willing to leave Electric Picnic for the game, I'll drive them back to Laois. It's not even a decision as far as I'm concerned. Honestly, there's at least 40 per cent of me that has the words of Nora Ephron ringing in my ear – 'Everything is copy' – and this drama has all the vital ingredients of an *Irish Times* column.

But the choice is stark for our lads. They've poured their hearts and souls into it, trained much harder than I have for the last eight months, and the key game of our entire season lands on the weekend when they've promised partners or pals that they're going to a music festival. I can't get angry at them, because I then become the emotional blackmailer of my nightmares, the crank, the unreasonable old bollocks ... I just wish they'd been given a different choice to the one they've got to make.

Wednesday, 31 August

Training since the Lucan game has been great. We still don't know who's going to the Electric Picnic and staying there; who's going, coming back for the game, and then returning; and who's just selling their ticket and staying home. There might be a few lads waiting until the last moment before telling friends and significant others they're pulling out, as I'd have done in the past, so we'll just see what the next seventy-two hours brings.

I went down to Dolphin earlier, a beautiful summer's evening, to watch our women's first team lose a county semi-final to Raheny by two points, in front of the biggest crowd I've ever seen in the place.

Saturday, 3 September

The Electric Picnic situation has been made clear to us. Two lads have sold their tickets, three lads are doing the full weekend, and three heroes are driving from Strad-bally back to Clontarf, playing the game, having a shower and then heading back to EP. (My chauffeuring services will not be required.)

I knew this on Friday morning, and by Friday night I had completely made my peace with it. And I couldn't believe the good grace with which everyone took it – it just really seemed like everyone knew instinctively that people did what they felt was the right thing to do in each instance, and I was really proud of how we'd handled it as a group, and how the management had handled it. What's the alternative? That you have fellas there who don't want to be there, or feel like football is something they are being forced to do? It can't be like that. It just can't. Not any more. And if we lose this game today, then so be it.

I was over to Clontarf in plenty of time and walked to the dressing room in a deluge. Five minutes later, and bang on schedule, the three boys walk in the door, wearing their wellies, their ponchos, and, most worryingly for them, their rather fragile wristbands, which are their tickets back into the festival.

This is our starting full-back, centre-back and mid-fielder. They're all twenty-two or younger, and my belief in the restorative qualities of extreme youth looks sure to be tested to the limit tonight. They seem basically all right, but the wellies don't leave much room for doubt about where they've been for the last twenty-four hours. We can only hope Clontarf have a few in the same position.

The game starts just as the rain begins to clear, and it's incredibly intense. I get a ball early, and whip over a nice score when I'm given a little more room than I'd normally expect. I hit a free wide that I should have gotten, and then hand over the left-sided frees to Conor, who hits his first one beautifully. I score the next free, but we concede a goal. I get a free just before half-time, we're down by three, and in my head I think having it down to a one-score game could be important. We win a forty-five and, from nothing, Olly Barrett gets a flick to it, and it's a goal. We're level, having not really played all that well, and we bounce over to the sideline.

We win the third quarter six points to one, with an exceptional fifteen minutes of football. We press up high on their kick-out, we squeeze the life out of them, and the game is pretty much ours at 1-11 to 1-5. Suddenly, out of nowhere, they get a penalty, score a couple of points. And then, confusion. The referee announces that the scores are level. Both sidelines had been shouting the correct scoreline onto the pitch, which had us one up, but the ref has it level. There's not much we can do, but now we're really hanging on. A draw will do us, but it's unbelievably tense. I get a point from play to put us one up, and then we hang on through eight minutes of injury time to get the win. It's just pure elation at the final whistle. Our three Electric Picnickers had been magnificent.

Decisions hadn't gone our way, we'd been caught on the hop, and yet we'd persevered. And the fact that we did it against Clontarf, who without doubt have had the wood on us in recent years, made it extra special.

In my first game against Clontarf, in 2018, their full-back had accused me of feigning injury after we'd gone up for a high ball against each other. His exact words were: 'Get up you diving bollocks, after all the giving out you do about the soccer lads on the radio.'

The night Dublin beat Galway in the All-Ireland semi-final that year, I met Jack McCaffrey outside the Stag's Head, who then introduced me to his brother Conor, who told me that he and a large proportion of his teammates on the Clontarf second team had signed up to the *Second Captains* World Service on the back of rumours that I'd told this story on the podcast, which I had.

We beat them in the league the following year, but in the Covid-shortened season of 2020 they beat us in the group stages of the junior championship, due in no small part to a horrific miss by me one-on-one with their keeper at a crucial juncture. I was so incredibly annoyed by that miss, and my lacklustre performance generally, that I'd barely noticed the fact that Dr Tony Holohan, TSS club member and at that moment probably the most famous man in the country, was acting as our umpire at that goal.

As I trudged disconsolately back to the sideline after the final whistle, replaying my one-on-one repeatedly in my head, Tony came up behind me and said tough luck, or some sympathetic words to that effect. I spat out a reply along the lines of 'luck had nothing to do with it, that was a fucking terrible miss' and jogged away from him. Given that this game might have been his sole respite from spearheading the fight against a deadly pandemic, this chance meeting might have been a great opportunity for me to achieve some perspective . . . an opportunity I spectacularly failed to take.

Clontarf they beat us again in the group stages of the junior championship in 2021, before we met them in that county final last November, when they were just a little too good for us. So I'd just never played well against them, and never really gotten a win that mattered against them. But this time we were through to the quarter-finals, and we'd done it the hard way.

The three lads had their showers and headed back down to Laois. The rest of us headed for the pub. It felt like a massive step had been taken.

Monday, 5 September

A foul-up in another championship group, which the county board failed to deal with properly, has delayed the entire competition by a fortnight. So we should be playing in two weeks' time, but it now leaves us with a month to train as the daylight hours decline and the temperature drops.

We've been in a good rhythm, and I feel like this could really disrupt us. I have also realized to my horror that, thanks to the delay in the championship, my holiday to Mexico at Hallowe'en begins on the day that our county final might well be played. I'd checked the fixtures before I'd booked that holiday and I'd been in the clear. And yet here we are again – the GAA will always find a way to screw you . . .

Tuesday, 6 September

. . . and now it gets worse. Austin Winston, the chair of Milltown GAA club, rang me today to tell me that the club are having a social at the end of next month, and at that social they're going to honour Dad for his forty years of work with the club. The date? 29 October . . . possibly the same day as the county final, and definitely the same day that I'm flying out to Mexico. This is literally beyond belief.

Thursday, 15 September
The Templeogue Synge Street social for 2022 has been announced, and it's set for 4 November . . . two days before I return home from Mexico. This is some kind of sick joke.

Saturday, 17 September
We should be playing our quarter-final today, but instead we're playing a challenge game against Crumlin. I kick an extraordinary amount of wides for one half of football, and get taken off at half-time to spare any further humiliation. But the delay hasn't worried us at all; in fact, it's given us a chance to build up our fitness, and maybe it'll prove to be the making of us.

Our quarter-final has been officially rearranged for 1 October, and it's the same day our vice-captain, Eamon Keegan, is getting married in Tipperary. He's obviously going to miss the game, but for the ten or twelve of us that have been invited, we're going to try to get the match played earlier in the day, to at least allow us to get down there in decent time. We live in hope.

Tuesday, 27 September
Before training. Championship week.

Ryan: 'Murph, what's the weather forecast like for the next week?'

Fergal Lonergan: 'Murph doesn't know everything, ye know. Just because he's old doesn't mean he's wise.'

Me: 'Are you only asking me because you think I might have a lawn to cut, so I keep an eye out for rain?' (This is, in fact, why I can correctly answer his question.)

Friday, 30 September
We tried all week to get the throw-in time put back a few hours to facilitate those of us attending Keego's wedding, to no avail. Then today, the death of Brian Mullins, a St Vincent's legend, was announced, and we were certain the game would be called off again. But the Mullins family have said that they don't want any games to be called off, so Vins played the senior camogie final tonight, and our game will go ahead as scheduled tomorrow. Those of us invited to Keego's wedding are getting a minibus to pick us up after the game and bring us directly to Tipperary for the afters of the wedding, and we're ready to rumble. The last month couldn't have gone much better from our point of view.

Saturday, 1 October
I wake up around 8 a.m. and I start to think about how strange indeed it is to be landing over to Vincent's home ground, barely twenty-four hours after Mullins's death was announced. I start to think maybe there's some way for us to honour the man, apart from the minute's silence.

I ring Bassy and see what he reckons. We come up with the idea of laying out one of Bassy's number 9 Dublin jerseys in front of us during the minute's silence, and I'm happy we've found something to mark the moment.

This is Vins' second team, and they'll always take the championship seriously – they're too good a club not to. And this is a quarter-final. So even if our league form was marginally better than theirs, I'm not expecting anything other than a dogfight.

I walk into full-forward before the throw-in, and I'm on a man I played with in my one season with Vincents in 2006. He can't quite believe it's sixteen years ago, and neither can I, quite frankly.

We start really well, and we're 4–2 up with about five minutes to go before half-time. They get a soft penalty, they stick that away, and then they get another goal, and from a position where we were in control, we're 2-3 to 0-4 down at half-time.

We're still right in this, but we need a quick start to the second half. I got three of the four points we scored in the first half, but I'd a couple of bad wides too, and when I'm off target with a free I probably should have gotten, I know I'm on borrowed time. I'm taken off with twenty minutes to go, and the change is at least partly the catalyst for us to get back within three . . . but two more quick-fire goals end the comeback.

There were no arguments – we were just beaten by a better team. Fiachra Breathnach, the former Galway player, came on for them with about twenty minutes to go, and I've a chat with him in the clubhouse bar afterwards for a minute. We grab ourselves a pint, and then it's out to the minibus for the trip to Tipp. We buy a few beers in the first off-licence we can find, and before long we're driving through the autumn dark across the country. No tears, no recriminations – just a slight nagging feeling that this journey, and this wedding, would have really been something if we'd managed to pull it out of the bag.

Wednesday, 5 October

We thought it was impossible for us to be promoted, given we'd have to beat Vincent's in our last league game by forty points to overtake Clann Mhuire on points difference. But the walkover we got off Skerries on my fortieth birthday means points difference can't be used to separate teams.

The winner of the match between the two teams involved is the next determining factor, but our game against Clann Mhuire was drawn. So, if we beat Vincent's, we'll have to play off against Clann Mhuire again just to see who finishes fourth and who will get into the *actual* promotion play-off against the team in third. So we'll take this week off, and then train once a week and wait for the county board to set a date for this fixture.

The likely scenario here is that both our final league game and, if we win that, the game against Clann Mhuire, will be played while I'm in Mexico. Unbelievable! It never ends! I'd be back for the final promotion play-off if we got there, I suppose. But it's unbelievable that I could miss a night honouring my father, two football games, and another club social, in one seven-day period out of the country . . . in November.

Thursday, 27 October

We've put two reasonable weeks of training in, even if attendance has dropped off a bit, and we're ready to play Vincent's on Saturday in our final league game . . . when the news comes through tonight that they're not in a position to field a team, giving us a walkover. So our game against Clann Mhuire to decide fourth place will be played on Sunday week . . . two hours after my flight home from Cancún is due to land.

Saturday, 5 November

My commute to the Clann Mhuire game begins at 10.30 a.m. Mexico time, with a taxi from our hotel (which I really, really didn't want to leave) to Cancún International Airport. In security, as I look around me, I suddenly see we're surrounded on all sides by the Westmeath senior footballers, who are returning home after their team holiday for winning the Tailteann Cup. Truly, you can go nowhere without running into the GAA.

Our first flight arrives in plenty of time in New York, and then we board our transatlantic flight home. It's taking off at 8 p.m. local time, scheduled to land in Dublin shortly after 8 a.m. The plan then is to race home, get my gear on, and be down at Dolphin Park at 9.30 ahead of a 10.30 throw-in.

Sunday, 6 November

By an insane stroke of luck, I was placed in an exit row on the flight from New York, with all the extra leg-room that comes with it. The flight lands ahead of schedule, and I'm home fifteen minutes sooner than I thought possible in even my most optimistic projections – early enough to pop down to the local café for a LARGE coffee. I feel pretty decent, even if I only got two hours of the sort of intermittent, mildly terrifying sleep that you only get on an aeroplane.

Then the warm-up begins.

I am completely spaced out. It's as if I'm floating about fifteen yards above the ground, watching myself fail to catch, kick or pass a ball. I'm obviously not starting, but now I think it's crazy to have even togged out at all.

I give myself a thorough warm-up again during half-time and I start to feel like maybe this could be OK. But we're seven points down and under severe pressure at the break. We make two substitutions at half-time, score two goals and a point inside five minutes, and all of a sudden we're level. Then we concede a goal. I come on with about fifteen minutes to go, and against all expectations, actually do OK. I kick three points from frees, and set up a couple of chances for goals that we can't quite finish. In the end we fall five points short. It's a bit of a sickener of a way to finish the year. We're not quite there. The season is over. But finishing fourth in our first full season as an AFL 4 team is a brilliant achievement.

We go into the dressing room for a debrief. Ray and Adrian tell us that they have been approached by the club to take over the senior team, and they've accepted the job. We expected this, and we wish them all the best. In amidst the hugs, and the earnest thanks for the hard work that we all did all year, the new manager for next year is announced. He's the man who took our under-17s all the way to a county 'A' semi-final earlier this month, and he's a brilliant appointment.

I look down and realize I haven't even taken my boots off. I'm not ready to leave it all behind. I see Diarmuid's partner Caitriona outside with their daughter. I see Michael Doherty and his new wife outside as well. I think about a fella coming up to manage his first adult team, with a cohort of young fellas he knows well from this year, all eager to discover if they can cut it in adult football. I think about what place a forty-year-old like me has in all that. I think about how I would approach this if I were in his shoes, how the club might want me to approach it. I linger in the car park, trying to bully our captain into organizing a night out for us in the next few weeks. On and on, I linger. I'm still not ready to leave.

Coda

After my 2022 club season finished, I spent a few weeks at home in Milltown with my parents working on this book. In the middle of October, I was sitting at the bar in Mullarkey's with Dad. I was flanked on my other side by John Waldron, and it just so happened that a couple of weeks after this night, my father and John would be the joint recipients of a Hall of Fame award from the club.

They had been told about the award well in advance, and so had plenty of time to figure out a list of people more deserving of the honour than they were. Drawing up that list was exactly what they were doing on that night in mid-October. Foremost in John's mind was Sean Brennan, the captain of the first Milltown team to win the county senior championship.

There's a photograph of Sean being presented with the Frank Fox Cup by then-Galway football board chairman Sean Purcell – often proclaimed, as we have heard, the best footballer of the twentieth century.

In the photo, Brennan looks almost impossibly handsome as he receives the trophy, an Elvis Presley mop of jet-black hair slick and wet from the day's rain. He holds the trophy at its middle with one hand, the reason for which becomes clear on closer inspection. His left jersey sleeve is empty at the wrist. He has only one hand.

I had known this fact about our first county-title-winning captain for my entire life. If you asked me that night last

October, I'd have said that he had emigrated as a young man and lost the hand in a cotton mill in Birmingham. (This is actually what happened to Michael Davitt, who founded the Land League in Irishtown, no more than three miles down the road from my location that night in Mullarkey's – funny the tricks your mind plays on you.)

But John was there, talking away to me about Sean Brennan, about what an exceptional footballer he was, that he came on in the All-Ireland semi-final of 1963 for Galway against Kerry, which I'd never known. And then John told me that for ten years after the accident that cost Sean his hand, he bent down and tied Sean's bootlaces before every game they played together.

That detail knocked me out. I couldn't stop thinking about it. I couldn't stop thinking either about how I'd always known about Sean's injury yet never really thought about it. Of course someone had to tie his bootlaces for him!

I met Sean a few months later. He's retired now, and lives in Caherlistrane, about fifteen miles from Milltown, and he told me the true story of what happened to his left hand as coolly and calmly as if he was talking about a scene from a movie.

On 18 March 1964, he was studying to be a priest in All Hallows College in Drumcondra. He had been the stage manager for a production of *Macbeth*, performed the day before, and on the day of the accident he was dismantling the set with four other students. One of them asked how they had created the big flash of fire in the famous witches' cauldron. To demonstrate, he poured magnesium powder onto a piece of cardboard, and someone held a match to it to cause the fire. Nothing happened, so Sean poured some more magnesium powder onto it. The can exploded in his hand.

The blood loss was extreme. One of the other students with him was his younger brother Gabriel, and he rushed Sean down to the infirmary, where his condition was so grave that he was given the last rites. He went to the Mater Hospital and was operated on that night. They amputated his arm from a point about halfway between his elbow and his wrist.

He was visited in the Mater by some priests from the college, but when he went from there to the National Rehabilitation Centre in Dun Laoghaire, no one came to see him for six weeks. He left the seminary and returned to Milltown that summer a physical wreck, with shrapnel still all over his body, and twelve stitches in an ugly wound on his neck that was millimetres from a main artery. He had lost two stone.

He went back to his parents' house. His mother had given birth to his youngest brother, Gerry, the day before the accident, and she was not informed of Sean's injury for a number of days, as it was felt she had enough to deal with. It was an unbearably traumatic time for his family. The village was devastated also. My aunt was a boarder in the Mercy Convent in Tuam that spring, in the same year as Sean's sister, and she remembers hearing about it and bursting into tears.

Sean was depressed, wrestling with the end of his college life (he said he would probably have left the seminary that summer in any case, but obviously not under such traumatic circumstances), and wrestling too with the idea of figuring out what he could do with the arm and the life he had left. He went to a tournament game the Milltown senior team were playing in south Mayo, and he overheard two men talking about 'young Brennan – the poor lad will never play again'.

That he was being talked about like this, in a county other than his own, is not surprising, because Sean was a genuinely top-level talent. He was still a student at All Hallows when he had been brought on as a substitute in that All-Ireland semi-final in 1963. Galway won that day, only to lose the final to Dublin, but they were about to embark on the most success-ful period of their entire history, and Sean, aged just twenty-one at the time, undoubtedly had the ability to have played his part.

Sean played alongside his clubmate and first cousin Noel Tierney in the Galway defence against Kerry on that day in 1963. Thirteen months later, Tierney was full-back again as Galway won the first of three All-Ireland titles in a row. That winter, while Sean recuperated, Tierney would be named the Texaco Footballer of the Year, the ultimate individual hon-our for a Gaelic footballer at that time. Sean was a huge supporter of that Galway team, and was at all those finals, but he admitted to shedding a tear or two as he saw them climb the steps of the Hogan Stand.

Whether inspired by the words of those men at the tour-nament game in south Mayo, by the success of his erstwhile Galway teammates, or by a drive that seemed fundamental to him, in that winter of '64 Sean started kicking a ball around at home, relearning how to play the game that he loved. An idea began to crystallize.

When the Milltown junior team were short a player for a game in the summer of 1965, he saw his chance. He walked into the dressing room, and no one said a word to him about his missing hand. He went out onto the field, and none of his opponents broached it with him, on that day or any other day.

He told me about the difficulties he faced during a game. The pain that shot through his body on the rare occasion he landed on the sharp point of his amputated forearm. The method he devised to pick up the ball in open play, scooping the ball from his left foot into his right hand, something he honed so expertly that he could lift the ball quicker than any two-handed player. The way any forward he ever marked automatically ran at his weak side when he was playing left corner-back, thoughtlessly heading out towards the sideline, where he could then hit them hard and fair over the line.

His story was written about a bit at the time, when Milltown won the 1971 county final. There was an article with him in one of the GAA periodicals of the era, a paragraph about him in the *Irish Echo* in America even. Bravery, resilience, dedication. These words all seem to fall far short of what he had shown.

He told me, in short, that football saved his life. If he could go back and play football, what was stopping him from doing anything else? He got a job with a construction company in Dublin, got married, had two kids. He moved down to north Galway in 1988. He now leads an almost picture-book ideal of country life with his lovely wife Mary. There is a polytunnel in the back yard, hens, and an extraordinary brightly coloured rooster, a beautiful golden pheasant, in a coop by the back door. He keeps bees and makes honey. Jam he makes from the strawberries in the polytunnel. The dog happily chasing around the place is called Mil, the Irish word for honey.

Mostly what I saw was a man now into his eighties who looked back on his football career with quiet pride and satisfaction. The photos of winning Milltown teams hang in his front hall, including the famous photo of him and Purcell with the Frank Fox trophy. He is one of the most self-assured, upbeat, sincere people I've ever met. It was genuinely a privilege to spend time in his house.

Believe it or not, I played senior football for Milltown with Sean Brennan's youngest brother, Gerry, the boy born the day before Sean's accident. Sean is twice my age now, and Gerry was twice my age when I first played with him, but we have that link. I haven't lived in Milltown for over two decades, and I've been resident in Dublin now for longer than I lived in the village I was born in. After all I've seen and lived through and loved and hated about the GAA (the emotional blackmail, the hypocrisy, the casual attitude to discipline, the self-congratulation), I can't get past that image of Sean in the dressing room, never needing to ask anyone for help as he got ready. Someone – John Waldron, or Pat Feerick, or one of his own brothers – was always there for him.

Acknowledgements

First of all, a very special thank you to my wonderful editor, Brendan Barrington, and to Michael McLoughlin at Sandycove, for approaching me with the idea of writing a book.

Go raibh míle maith agaibh to my handsome, youthful colleagues in *Second Captains*, Eoin McDevitt, Ken Early, and Simon Hick, for their understanding throughout the last eighteen months. And a special thank you to my great friend Mark Horgan for all the laughs, and for your counsel and advice through the years.

Thank you to Sinéad O'Carroll for your invaluable input, and to Paul Flynn, Jamie Wall, Dylan Haskins, Adrian O'Flynn, Hugh Ormond, and Paul Rouse for reading early drafts of a number of chapters.

To Collie McKeown, Clare Henderson, and Sorcha Pollak for being such enthusiastic writing (and reading) co-conspirators, and to Colin Doyle and Pauline Vincey for their constant friendship.

A few passages in this book first appeared in my column in the *Irish Times*. Thanks to the paper for the opportunity to write about the GAA every week, and to Malachy Logan, Noel O'Reilly, and Malachy Clerkin in particular.

Thanks to the wonderful people at Templeogue Synge Street GFC, who have given this old wreck another trip or two around the circuit.

To every single player I ever shared a Milltown team with: we were small, but we were mighty. And we'll stay that way. And a heartfelt thanks to the people of Milltown, particularly to those in the village who do so much for my father since he was diagnosed with Parkinson's. Words genuinely fall short.

To my extended family in Waterford, Dublin, Clare, and Galway, in particular my uncles Jim and Noel; and to Brian, Paul, John, Tony, and Fran for being such lunatics about all this. I will say that I had no choice in the matter.

And to Gill – for your unstinting support in this, and all things . . . even in your moments of general bewilderment.